# Praying Dangerously

## Other Books by Regina Sara Ryan

*The Wellness Workbook: How to Achieve Enduring Health &
Vitality,* with John W. Travis, M.D.

*Simply Well: Choices for a Healthy Life,* with John W. Travis,
M.D.

*After Surgery, Illness or Trauma: 10 Steps to Renewed Energy
and Health*

*No Child in My Life*

*Everywoman's Book of Common Wisdom,* with Erica Jen and
Lalitha Thomas

*The Woman Awake: Feminine Wisdom for Spiritual Life*

*Praying Dangerously: Radical Reliance on God,* first edition

*Breastfeeding: Your Priceless Gift to Your Baby and Yourself,*
with Deborah Auletta, IBCLC

*Only God: A Biography of Yogi Ramsuratkumar*

*Igniting the Inner Life*

# *Praying Dangerously*

## RADICAL RELIANCE ON GOD

*10th Anniversary Edition*

REGINA SARA RYAN

HOHM PRESS • *Prescott, Arizona*

Design and layout by Kadak Graphics, www.kadakgraphics.com

ISBN: 978-1-935387-20-6

The Library of Congress has catalogued this 10^{TH} Anniversary Edition as follows:

Ryan, Regina Sara
    Praying dangerously: radical reliance on God / Regina Sara Ryan
        p. cm
    Includes bibliographical references and index.
    ISBN 1-890772-06-2 (pbk)
        1.    Prayer—Christianity. I. Title

BV210.2 R92 2001
291.4'3—dc21                                                                 2001039421

Excerpt from "East Coker" in FOUR QUARTETS, copyright 1940 by T.S. Eliot and renewed 1968 by Esme Valerie Eliot, reprinted by permission of Houghton Mifflin Harcourt Publishing Company.

Excerpts from *The Kabir Book*, by Robert Bly, Copyright © 1971, 1977 by Robert Bly; © by the Seventies Press. Reprinted by permission of Beacon Press, Boston.

HOHM PRESS
P.O. Box 2501
Prescott, AZ 86302
800-381-2700
http://www.hohmpress.com

This book was printed in the U.S.A. on acid-free paper using soy ink.

*In praise and gratitude to my guides in prayer*

*Lee Lozowick and Yogi Ramsuratkumar*

# CONTENTS

# Praying Dangerously

Deliver us, O God, O Truth, O Love, from quiet prayer
from polite and politically correct language,
from appropriate gesture and form
and whatever else we think we need to invoke or to praise You.

Let us instead pray dangerously—
wantonly, lustily, passionately.
Let us demand with every ounce of our strength,
let us storm the gates of heaven, let us shake up ourselves
and our plaster saints from the sleep of years.

Let us pray dangerously.
Let us throw ourselves from the top of the tower,
let us risk a descent to the darkest region of the abyss,
let us put our head into the lion's mouth
and direct our feet to the entrance of the dragon's cave.

Let us pray dangerously.
Let us not hold back a little portion,
dealing out our lives—our precious minutes and our
energies—like some efficient accountant.
Let us rather pray dangerously—naked, unsafe, wasteful!

Let us ask for nothing less than the Infinite to ravage us.
Let us ask for nothing less than annihilation in the
Fires of Love
Let us not pray in holy half-measures nor walk the middle path
for too long,
but pray madly, foolishly.
Let us be too ecstatic,
let us be too overwhelmed with sorrow and remorse,
let us be undone, and dismembered and gladly.

Left to our own devices, ah what structures of deceit we
have created;
what battlements erected, what labyrinths woven, what traps
set for ourselves, and then fallen into.
Enough.
Let us pray dangerously—hot prayer, wet prayer, fierce
prayer, fiery prayer, improper prayer, exuberant prayer,
drunken and completely unrealistic prayer.

Let us say Yes, again and again and again.
and Yes some more.
Let us pray dangerously,

the most dangerous prayer is *Yes*.

# INTRODUCTION
*To the 10<sup>th</sup> Anniversary Edition*

Readers of the first edition of this book (published in 2001) were enthusiastic in their praise, calling it a brave and useful book. Prayer groups and church congregations around the U.S. have used it for study, and it has been translated into Dutch, German and French.

The message of *Praying Dangerously* is more relevant now than it was ten years ago. The world has changed radically since 2001. As more people worldwide candidly admit to their reliance on prayer, the attention to this subject has dramatically increased each year. War, economic instability, environmental and weather-related disasters—many factors draw us inward or back to our churches. In prayer groups and retreats of all kinds we are looking for comfort and consolation, for spiritual direction, or for answers to the eternal questions that have always challenged humanity.

*Praying Dangerously* instructs us that we can *grow up* spiritually, leaving behind a childish relationship to prayer as a superstitious ritual or mere plea for favors. It encourages us to recognize the difference between prayer that asks only for reassurance, and prayer that asks for God and stands for transformation. It invites us to assume greater responsibility for our inner lives by *choosing* the "not-knowing," the insecurity, the difficult circumstances as potential blessings and means of purification and inspiration. We can cease being "victims" of God's Will, while at the same time embracing genuine surrender and reliance on the irrefutable power of love.

This 10th anniversary edition is fully revised, with several completely new sections including: Radical Reliance on God; Praise and Prayer; Alchemical Prayer; and a new chapter titled "Praying on the Subway," about how our travels and other activities in public places can provide us with a constant impetus for blessing others.

*Praying Dangerously* draws from many sources and many traditions, from the Orthodox Christian classic *The Philokalia*, to the writings of ancient Sufi saints—Rabi'a, Rumi and Abil-Kheir—to contemporary treatments of prayer by Thomas Merton, Thomas Keating and others. *This book* expands the possibilities of prayer, invites a renewal of the inner life, and inspires us to abandon superficial, safe notions of prayer in favor of the Real.

## WHAT IS PRAYER?

We are all spiritually hungry, and some of us are starving, as evidenced by the huge market for the nearly four hundred books written on the subject of prayer every year in the U.S. alone. We crave substantial nourishment—a source of food for the inner systems that don't get fed by meat or potatoes. Relationship with God *is* that food. Truth is that food. The pure reality of life, just as it is, is that food. Praying involves us in all phases of this food cycle—the planting, the watering, the waiting, the pruning, the harvesting, the cooking and the eating … ultimately, the *communion* with That which we know, intuitively, will complete us, although we may have no words for this.

As simple and straightforward as food cultivation and food preparation may be, it is also a miraculous and mysterious process of the highest order. To garden, for example, is to participate in the very act of creation, serving that mystery to the best of our ability, while surrendering our own timing to the timing of the earth. To pray is much the same. It involves us in the mystery that is God, love, life or truth, demanding from us both action and surrender. To pray is to cultivate a love affair with love itself, the most awesome power in creation. Hence the title, *Praying Dangerously*.

This book is written for those who are ready, without naiveté, to enter more deeply into the miracle and the mystery of relationship with the Divine. It is for those who are hungry to engage prayer as a way of life, rather than an occasional hobby. *Praying Dangerously* is for the man or woman willing to approach the thick "cloud of unknowing" that surrounds the peak of this mountain of mystery, without turning back; ready to risk the "annihilating fire," the "all-consuming love," or any other awesome and devastating description of union with God that the mystics of all ages have left us. As such, praying dangerously is an activity for grown-ups, warriors, adventurers, passionate lovers, not for petulant children who will only be happy when they are getting their own way, dominating the attention of others, manipulating their parents into submission. We have all been such children in relationship to God, praying as a type of demand and then becoming hostile, blaming or withdrawn, when things don't turn out the way we intended. There is nothing to be ashamed of in this behavior, as everybody needs to grow up, and "God can take it!" as Elisabeth Kübler-Ross, the great pioneer in grief and loss, has said. Nonetheless, it is a far cry from the union with the Beloved to which we are heirs.

*Praying Dangerously* is an invitation to expand the possibilities of prayer within our lives, elevating our desire for personal comfort, security, satisfaction and prosperity to that of a fierce and awesome commitment to life—a commitment to serve and surrender ... "to love, honor, cherish and obey" in whatever way is most obviously needed, moment to moment, within this mystery, this "Great Process of Divine Evolution," as my teacher Lee Lozowick would say, regardless of personal cost. *Praying Dangerously* is ultimately about a celebration of the highest potentials of the human soul—love, gratitude, communion, selfless service, worship and adoration. Those who pray dangerously sing with the poet Goethe who wrote, "I praise what is truly alive, what longs to be burned to death."

## How I Came To Write This Book

Writing this book about prayer has kept me praying. The blessed curse of the writer is that their subject becomes an obsession during the time of their research and writing. What a gift to be forced to see and evaluate everything from the perspective of prayer—to find prayer in everything, and everything as potential prayer. As I wrote the first and now the second edition of this book I've listened to every conversation I've had with other people waiting to hear something that would inspire the next essay. I've read books about prayer that have thrilled me and some that have made be laugh. I've grappled with the question of just what prayer *is* as I've wandered the hills above my home, or as I've cleaned the walls of a bathroom in a dilapidated house with broken plumbing. Driving along the highway with unsuspecting friends, I've asked them what *they* would be grateful to find in a book about prayer.

And then I've locked up their answers in my heart, awaiting the sacred moment when I'd entrust the words to paper.

I've come to a few startling conclusions, and felt a tremendous sense of blessedness along the way. The process has been its own reward. This is the book I was looking for forty years ago, and the book I need today when a ringing telephone rather than remembrance of purpose starts my day. If I have one wish, or prayer, for this book it is that it begs to be put down because the reader has become inspired to pray instead of read.

My friends think I know something about prayer. Even my spiritual teacher said the same. "You have a rich prayer life," he advised me when I started this book, "write from that." I trust his words, even though I often feel like I am flailing around in the confusion of mind when I sit down to prayer. Thank goodness that I've learned at least one thing well over the years, which is that prayer doesn't depend on a peaceful mind.

Actually, I used to know a lot more about prayer than I do now. After all, I've been praying all my life, and at least part of that life as a nun in a Roman Catholic convent. I've also been practicing within the tradition of my spiritual teacher for over twenty-five years. I spend a reasonable amount of time in prayer each day, both at home and in a meditation hall with others who share my teacher's tradition. I often tell my friends and family that I will "keep them in my prayers," and I do. I love to pray. But, quite frankly, as the years have unfolded I have realized more and more that I am the beginner of the beginners—a mystic in diapers. And, I recommend such a place to others, since it helps greatly to relieve the tendency to spiritual pride that can so easily become associated with one's prayer. Maybe my experience can be of service to others who feel the holy longing, yet find themselves so often in the dark.

# RAW PRAYER

My teacher's approach to prayer was largely unspoken. In all my years with him, as I remember, he formally addressed the subject on maybe a dozen occasions, and that generally quite briefly. Nonetheless, my own process of prayer, and the content of what I call prayer today is soaked through with his influence. He was during his life, and still is, a guide in the path of prayer—a guidance that he effected in silence, in stillness, in a dropped clue or a shared glance in the chambers of prayer that he set up for group participation, and in the inner listening he encouraged. My teacher was a master of sensitivity and discrimination in the domain of spiritual life and practice. Slowly, almost imperceptibly, he helped me to distinguish the voice of the Beloved, the whiff of the Beloved, from the meandering of ego's imagination and the cloying smell of bliss. Some of this discrimination has been hard earned.

One summer evening in the late 1990s, my friend Debbie asked my teacher a few questions about prayer that she and I had been discussing. Before he talked about prayer, however, he talked about me. "Regina has a genuine vocation to prayer," he said, "but she sometimes confuses it with her sentimental and romantic notions about the subject."

Hearing this, I was both intrigued and deeply grateful. Certainly he had given me a left-handed compliment of the highest degree, but he had also given me another challenge to work with. That warning about sentimentality continues to gnaw at my bones. It continues to spoil my fun, as it hangs over my head like a date of termination. Consequently, I treasure it, as I treasure the constancy of my teacher's commitment to my awakening from the dream of separation from God, and to my potential as a woman of prayer. That indictment has demanded a radical re-examination of the context of my approach to prayer. It has been another push in the direction of unlearning all that I thought I knew about the subject, which I see as a constant in this process. It has inspired my prayer and leant urgency to my quest for the truth, beyond the illusory and the feel-good. Raw prayer, real prayer, prayer beyond romance and sentimentality, dangerous and fiery and difficult and painful prayer that seals the bond between lovers and keeps the love alive—that is what this book is about.

## PUT THIS BOOK DOWN AND PRAY

What prayer actually *is* cannot be written. And all the words you will read about prayer, here or anywhere, are worth nothing unless you put the books down and begin to live out what you ache to live, and what the words are inviting.

When you do put the book away, however, you will wonder why prayer seemed so obvious, so clear, so desirable when you read about it in neat lines of black type on off-white paper. And why, when you settled down to pray at long last, the words suddenly lost their clarity or their impact. You may find yourself hungering for the communion that you know is possible through prayer, yet that communion eludes you. You find yourself jealous of those who seem to have accomplished something in the domain of prayer, and wonder how they managed it. Comparing yourself to these others, you may be disheartened. You aren't getting the results that the books promise, or at least point to. So, mired in the labyrinth of mind, you might be tempted to throw the baby out with the bath water. You may decide to skip the whole thing.

On the other hand, if you are one of the intrepid you may

stiffen your upper lip and plunge into the fray, ready to do battle with your mind. You may decide that you are going to get the goods, no matter what, as if praying was some contest.

Either way, however, you lose—which is not to say don't attempt it, everybody loses a lot in this path. In the first case, forgetting the whole thing, you end the journey before it is begun. In the second instance, despite the fact that a disciplined mind is one prerequisite to prayer, that discipline must be held with great tenderness and sensitivity. You lose if you are arming yourself for lovemaking. Steeled. Fortified. How could one ever experience the loving communion of relationship with Divinity from such a rigid posture?

So, this process of prayer in which we are engaged must be appreciated as a sojourn into a mystery, into a domain that is boggling to the mind and necessarily so. And the bad news is that in most cases, which means for most of us, the mind is boggled by the mind being boggled. That means, the mind is undone by being boggled, frustrated, bored, confused, not by some brilliant flash of light illuminating the path and burning all muddiness away, even though for some lucky souls that actually happens. Halleluia!

We live out the journey of prayer. We live it out by walking it day in and day out. We stammer our way through prayer, the way children stutter when they are learning to talk. We stumble our way through prayer, the way children trip and lose balance as they are learning to walk. But the important thing is that we don't give up and decide never to talk or walk again just because we are making more missteps or saying funny or foolish things that leave the grown-ups around us in hysterical laughter. And we don't rigidify ourselves, trying to talk by only saying perfectly pronounced words, or trying to walk like a perfect little soldier, and punishing ourselves when we make a mistake.

To learn to pray is a bit like learning a new language to-gether with a whole new set of protocols or customs of a foreign culture. We will never learn the language unless we are willing to speak it, or travel around and attempt to put into practice the protocol that the book is telling us about. One can starve that way! At some point you simply have to risk being a fool and try to say the new words. And, you have to give yourself the time to absorb the new customs—like you might in visit-ing Japan, when seeing people bowing to one another day in and day out for months, all of a sudden you are bowing too.

So it is with prayer. You put yourself in the culture of prayer and immerse yourself in its environment, but you also give yourself time each day, and perhaps many times a day, when you simply experiment with this new language, which is often not a language at all, but a listening.

Trust the intuition, the hunger, the desire for prayer that has carried and directed you thus far. Julian of Norwich, a great Christian mystic of the fourteenth century, advised that the worst hindrance to spiritual development was the failure to trust that what God had begun in us would be brought to completion by God as well. Prayer has begun.

## HOLY LONGING

Tell a wise person, or else keep silent,
because the massman will mock it right away.
I praise what is truly alive,
What longs to be burned to death.

In the calm water of the love-nights,
Where you were begotten, where you have begotten,
A strange feeling comes over you
When you see the silent candle burning.

Now you are no longer caught
in the obsession with darkness,
and a desire for higher love-making
Sweeps you upward.

Distance does not make you falter.
Now, arriving in magic, flying,
And finally, insane for the light,
You are the butterfly and you are gone.

And so long as you haven't experienced
This to die and so to grow
You are only a troubled guest
On the dark earth.

      —Goethe[1]

# I

# TRANSFORMATIONAL PRAYER

This book is not primarily about conversational or dialogic prayer. Plenty of others have offered wonderful instruction in prayer of this type, and some of their words will be reiterated here. *Praying Dangerously* is also not essentially about inspiration, help, or comfort—the familiar content of many prayers. Therefore, it is not ultimately about achieving greater peace and harmony, or even greater courage and kindness, although these side effects of prayer will generally be observable in those who pray.

The basic distinction in what I call dangerous prayer is brilliantly articulated by author and teacher Ken Wilber, but has been made by many other pioneers in spiritual life before him. Wilber explains two functions of religion or spiritual life, and consequently two approaches to the path. The first function of religion is *translational*, he says. We *translate* our lives into a different language, so to speak. Whereas before we may have been cruel, violent, totally self-serving, addicted and proud, religion helps us to translate our old values, behaviors and belief systems. Now we begin to speak a language of kindness, substituting service for self-obsession; we clean up our addictive acts and start giving our kids the attention they deserve. We use our prayer and our participation in ritual and service as a means of bringing harmony, where previously there was only chaos and insanity. Instead of thinking that we are the be all and end all of our own existence, we are subsequently placed properly within the context of creaturehood, or stewardship to the earth.

Applying this distinction to prayer, I assert that *translational* prayer is about helping us to adjust. It is about peace and consolation, and support in going through the hard times. It is about teaming up with God in order to get better. It is about learning to accept the inevitable. As Wilber says, it is about strengthening and shoring up the ego (the self-sense), helping it to become and remain functional.

Most writing about prayer, especially the popularized treatments of our time, deals with this translational level or function of prayer. And this is good. Such prayer is necessary. The world is going to hell in a handbasket and prayer helps us to find our way in the midst of the disintegration around us. With our functional lives in order, with God on our side in the truest sense of the term, we can negotiate for peace. We can bring some sanity to the office in the morning, and some patience home to our kids at night. We can carve out the time within our hectic schedules to create silence and solitude in order to commune with nature, with the heart of life, with God. We can examine our consciences and become better people who are no longer legitimized in dropping nuclear weapons on their enemies, or nailing each other's children to their front doors. God help us; God help the world; we need to pray!

Translational prayer is invaluable. It is a necessary stage. And it goes quite far—which is why most people who pray participate in this type of prayer for all their lives. Yet, the fact remains that it is not the only function of religion, nor the only type of prayer, whether that translational prayer takes the form of praise, thanksgiving or petition.

Religion in so far as it is a source of consolation is a
hindrance to true faith.           —Simone Weil[2]

I will call the other function of religion or spiritual life,
as Wilber does, *transformational*. In this domain, the rules of
the previous game don't apply. Transformation is a whole new
venture. Far from aiming at peace, transformational prayer
aims at the sword. Far from feeling better, the soul that is
"transformationally prayed" is being annihilated, consumed,
eaten up and spit out. The self or ego that, in the course of
translational prayer, is dismantled and rearranged in a new
and clearer syntax, is now wiped out. It no longer has the least
say in the play. With transformational prayer the separate self
has been subsumed by what is larger, or truer, or higher (if you
will), or wholly (holy) Other. Transformational prayer is about
death to all our notions of God, prayer, holiness, spiritual life,
and satisfaction or peace. Only in such death or annihilation is
a real life possible … or so say the mystics and great poets, and
scores of wise elders and saints throughout the ages.

In speaking of a transformation of the self (the small "self"),
I am not referring to what is popularly called a "flow experience"
wherein one is so absorbed in the task at hand that the sense
of ego-identity is temporarily lost. All types of art, sport, lovemaking and creative expression demonstrate this—even those
that are completely motivated by a desire for power, prestige and
self-serving pleasure. Such "flow" may all still be a function of
ego. Neither is this transformation necessarily a peak experience or a bliss state, nor a condition characterized by service in
its traditional forms, or by gentleness or attractiveness to others. No. When I point to transformation, I am referencing the
teaching and example of my teacher, indicating something to-
tal—complete and permanent—and so unique to the individual

undergoing it as to be relatively unpredictable. Ego as we know it will not survive this transformation. As Wilber puts it:

> For authentic transformation is not a matter of belief but of the death of the believer; not a matter of translating the world but of transforming the world; not a matter of finding solace but of finding infinity on the other side of death. The self is not made content; the self is made toast.[3]

"I" cannot lay claim to such a complete transformation. Nonetheless, *Praying Dangerously* is not essentially about solace, cool detachment, contentment. Rather, the fiery and dangerous prayer I explore here is a prayer wherein the prayer literally begs for a type of death, and for the excruciating increase of desire, intensity, and longing for the Truth, or God, or the Beloved, or the One, or the Self, or the Good ... many terms point to the same ultimate reality. Prayer, as I have come to appreciate it, is not about cooling our desires, but about adding fuel to the fire of our longing. Increasing our longing is how we generate spiritual heat—internally and externally. And only with heat can we be cooked, that is, transformed.

> A chickpea leaps almost over the rim of the pot
> where it's being boiled.
> "Why are you doing this to me?"
> The cooks knocks it down with the ladle.
> "Don't you try to jump out.
> You think I'm torturing you,
> I'm giving you flavor,
> so you can mix with spices and rice
> and be the lovely vitality of a human being ...
>                                                     —Rumi[4]

Transformational prayer, therefore, is an alchemical process. We get cooked in prayer into a tasty stew. Then we get served up for supper to whomever or whatever is in need of feeding in the moment—be that God, or some wayfaring angel, or our neighbor down the street ... it's not up to us to decide, anyway.

"When the Guest is being searched for, it is the intensity of the longing for the Guest that does all the work. Look at me, and you will see a slave of that intensity," wrote Kabir, a mystic poet of the fifteenth century.[5] Because we are less concerned here with satisfaction, with peace, with harmony, with feeling good, this prayer will often be hot prayer, fiery prayer. This is the prayer that, once tasted, will keep the body aching for more, hungering, crying out to the great mystery, or attempting to pierce the cloud of unknowing with a "sharp dart of longing love."[6] And it will be dangerous prayer. Any path of prayer, whether translational or transformational, will certainly change one's life. Isn't that precisely why people pray in the first place—to effect change? So often we pray because we want a better job, or because we want healing from an illness, or we want safety rather than insecurity for our kids. But, this is not the change I am talking about here. I call prayer dangerous because it has the potential to destroy the entire underpinning of ego's security. Prayer splits the atoms of our cells. And when the atoms are split ... well, there is no polite way to handle a nuclear reaction.

The Sufi master Irina Tweedie, quoting an early Christian mystic, described the path of love, or what we might call spiritual work, as "a bridge of hair across a chasm of fire."[7] Funny, but I used to imagine a thin and dangerous traverse, from which, without extreme caution and diligence one could fall and be burned up at any moment. The analogy was a call to practice. Today, however, in the light of praying dangerously, I see that a bridge of hair across a chasm of fire is sure death from the git'go. Such a bridge cannot exist for more than a few moments. It will ignite—perhaps in ten seconds, perhaps thirty, but ignite it will. And when it does, whomever or whatever happens to be attached to it at the time will be incinerated. So, why are these people lining up to cross it?

One would think that this type of death and annihilation would be the least desirable circumstance in the cosmos, perhaps second only to the varieties of torture inflicted by one race or nation of humans on another. Yet, for all these painful descriptions, let's face it, some of us want it! An inner urgency draws us to this type of prayer like a moth to a candle flame, unless we have deliberately blinded our eyes to the light. Something in us longs to die, as Goethe expressed it, in order that it may know a higher lovemaking. It is to these hungry lovers that this book is addressed.

Certainly this is not the first book on transformational prayer. *The Philokalia*, written between the fourth and the fifteenth centuries by spiritual masters of the Orthodox Christian tradition, covered the subject quite thoroughly. The Sufi mystics—both men and women—have poured forth their longing for annihilation in love, in poetry and in treatises on prayer. And in our own times, Thomas Merton, Chagdud Tulku, Vendana Mataji, Rabbi Zalman Schachter-Shalomi and many others from various world traditions, have done their fair share of promotion. Nonetheless, genuine transformation, as indicated by Wilber's definition, is as extremely rare a phenomenon in our day as it has ever been, despite the claims of contemporary popularizers of spiritual life who seem to think that just because more people are talking about transformation, they are somehow "getting it." In my experience, however, although teachings *about* transformation are readily available, I find that their context is more often askew or entirely lost, and their content is fast being co-opted, sweetened into a palatable mush, and served up on the pages of spiritual books and magazines, on CDs, and in the brochures that advertise the seminars and workshops that proliferate on the spiritual scene. So much that is considered spiritual life or work these days is so much picnicking at the edge of the chasm. The picnickers frolic with endless fascinations—like the new insights they are constantly having about their psychological problems; the archetypal dreams they had last night and now need to analyze; the powerful new seminars that have just come to town. Our satisfaction with this mush is what dulls our senses, leading us to believe that we are indeed heading for the toaster, when in fact we are actually putting another protective lock on the breadbox.

In effect, the sweetening of the path of transformation—through watering down the nature of sacrifice and surrender—leaves us with the idea that we can pray while keeping ourselves intact, thus avoiding the fire of annihilation. Such sweetening confines all our efforts in the spiritual domain to the lighting of an occasional votive candle, rather than leading us into the center of the firestorm that the great spiritual teachers and masters have been setting for centuries.

## MAKING IT NICE

Nearly thirty-five years ago, sitting in *darshan* with the outspoken and infamous guru Bhagwan Shri Rajneesh at his Poona, India ashram, I heard voiced a type of spiritual heresy that has remained a source of irritation ever since. It happened shortly after Mother Teresa was awarded the Nobel Prize for Peace.

"If Jesus was alive today," the Indian holy man drawled, his face smiling, "*he* would never have been given the Nobel Prize." In so many words, Rajneesh reminded his listeners that Jesus was a radical witness to something that the "world" could never accept. Jesus' words and his life demonstrated a type of crazy wisdom that would always be misunderstood by the masses.

It took me years of gnawing on that bit of insight to recognize, for myself, that giving Mother Teresa the Nobel Prize said more about the culture awarding it than it did about the individual receiving it. What appeared as a long-overdue gesture of acknowledgement, the crowning achievement from the perspective of translational religion, might very well be an unconscious attempt on ego's part to legitimize and thereby warp the relentless edge of the sword that Mother Teresa wielded throughout her life. After all, granting some famous person entry into "the club" is tremendously reassuring and comforting to the egos of the other members. The illusion is strengthened that with such acknowledgment we have paid our dues or paid our respects. We feel good about the Nobel Prize going to such a worthy recipient, and something in us relaxes. "Maybe things are getting better," we think. "Maybe the world isn't on the brink of destruction," we speculate.

Let's face it, it is much easier to praise Mother Teresa than to follow her example; as it is much more comforting to read a book on prayer than to pray.

The current phenomenon surrounding the thirteenth-century mystic poet and spiritual teacher Rumi provides another example. The club of Rumi lovers throughout the world is growing daily. Translations of his poems fill a sizeable shelf in many large bookstores. Quotations from his work appear in advertisements for all sorts of popular workshops. One large greeting-card company even approached a well-known translator seeking to make a deal for a whole line of Rumi greetings, which the translator refused to allow, much to his credit.

Popularity aside, Rumi's message has always been about ruin, or *fana* (annihilation) as the Sufis refer to it. Rumi was toast. After the death of his beloved teacher, Shams-i Tabriz—whom legend recounts was murdered by Rumi's jealous students—the once-renowned professor Rumi could no longer win in the old ways. His poems are dangerous and fiery prayers that speak of divine madness and drunkenness—a loss of all that he formerly held as sacred and identifiable as self. Even his students turned against him. Absorbed and lost in love, he composed 30,000 verses of heartbreaking poetry about the love that does such things:

> First, He pampered me with a hundred favors,
> Then melted me with the fire of sorrows.
> After He sealed me with the seal of Love,
> I became Him.
> Then, He threw my self out of me.
>
> —Rumi[8]

Quite obviously, this world of contemporary culture is not about approving the annihilation of the self-sense. In fact, quite the opposite. Rumi's poems have been set to music and sold as aphrodisiacs. It was only a matter of time. Those of us committed to the cultivation of the inner life are well advised to keep this in mind.

## KEEPING PRAYER PURE

For ages, persons of advanced spiritual wisdom have recognized this tendency of the culture at large to legitimize, dilute and thus distort the genuine transformational teachings. To preserve the purity of such teachings they have attempted to hide or mask them. In many cases these wise teachers have rendered the teachings inaccessible, except to the few seekers who could successfully navigate an ocean of obstacles to prove themselves worthy of the transmission. The gurus have hung out on the mountaintops for other reasons than to be closer to heaven. They have tried to keep the genuine teachings out of the hands of the advertising media.

In the tradition of the Bauls of Bengal, India, an itinerant sect of ecstatic singers, dancers and lovers of God, the revered teacher Monaha Khépa deliberately kept the road to his hut so full of ruts that even a skilled bicyclist could not take it. As one of his disciples described, the dirt floor of Monaha's dwelling was so uneven that it was not possible to place down one teacup without spilling it. The Bauls have typically refused to commit their *dharma* (doctrine, practice) to writing, preferring to keep it in the oral tradition and "in the body," as a way of keeping it from harm. Only by initiation from a Baul guru could the would-be aspirant receive the truth.

Bringing the smell of the toast closer to home, my own spiritual teacher demonstrated a public persona that was easily dismissed as decidedly unspiritual. His street-wise language and confrontive teaching style, his sometimes unconventional dress (second-hand t-shirts, sweat pants and sandals), his beaded dreadlocks, together with his willingness to insult the sleepwalking behavior that has become the cultural norm, could generally be counted on to clear a room of curiosity seekers in record time. Those who left his lectures early, annoyed or simply dumbfounded, often judged him a fool. Those who stayed sometimes assigned him to the role of entertainer, much like the king's jester who possessed the awesome responsibility of ridiculing pretense. While the crazy-wise teacher may be a source of endless fascination, he or she will usually attract a much more meager following.

Although my teacher didn't publicly declare it, I surmise that his activities were a conscious practice in the art of losing face, and a deliberate attempt to discourage the merely curious. Like his Bengali Baul ancestors, he knew that the teaching was easily corrupted. He knew that as long as one was legitimized by the good opinions of others, one was always less free to break the rules, or to step outside the lines. Losing face is a means whereby one plugs in the toaster.

## WHAT DO WE DO?

Let us keep in mind, even as we open a new book on prayer, that we are all indictable for the legitimizing of spirituality. There is no way around it. This is ego's job. It wants to maintain safety and hence survival. It wants predictability. We are not bad for this, but we may be stupid.

Furthermore, I make a case for the recognition that all the judgments we have about what is spiritual, and what is not, are all colored by our cultural mindset, dulled by malnourishment due to the mush we have eaten for so long. When Christ raised a man from the dead on the Sabbath he was categorically condemned by the legitimate religious authorities for violating the law. I recently gave a talk to a group of women and told the story of Irina Tweedie, the respected Sufi master mentioned earlier, who was given her teacher's mantle of responsibility, and who carried on the work of transformational spirituality for about thirty years. When I got to the part of the story in which her master treated her coldly and even ignored her for months on end as a part of her initiation, one of my listeners, a minister of a Protestant sect, exclaimed: "Christ would never have done that!" I couldn't respond. There was no way to offer this woman a way out of or through her tight little definition of what spiritual life and practice was all about. She was even using the example of her own master, Jesus, legitimizing him as the model of kindness and gentleness as a means of discrediting the actions of another. How quickly we forget that a master such as Jesus had told his contemporaries that they were a bunch of "whitened sepulchres" (today we might say "whitewashed rot") and that he had come to bring not peace but the sword.

While it is the necessary function of translational religion to break down the teachings into understandable chunks so that they can be chewed, swallowed and digested, thereby giving coherency and meaning to our lives, we need to remain open to the transformational possibilities inherent in insecurity, confusion, paradox, the "beginner's mind,"[9] the ways of "not-knowing."

Let's face it, for all intents and purposes the rational mind has triumphed—the status quo *is* one of reason, regimentation and safety. We will, therefore, continue to reject what disturbs us. We will try to rationalize this rejection with polite explanations. We will still look for religious models who meet our standards—standards approved by the ego—and for words of prayer that promise us the smooth path, the easy road. We will be legitimate, but we will have lost.

Underworld manifestations and their interface with spirituality (and in this case prayer) are particularly hard to accept.

While we may not refuse the self-understanding present in times of great loss and pain, we are less likely to acknowledge the transformational elements present in eroticism, strong emotions, politically incorrect displays of any kind, drunkenness, violence (even the stick that the Zen teacher typically administered to sleepy meditators has been called into serious question in our times), and other behaviors. Yet, as our transformed predecessors have reminded us, the kingdom of heaven will not be taken except by storm! On the other hand, but also to the same point, try referring to that storm with words like obedience, surrender, submission, even devotion and sacrifice, and watch the people around you squirm.

Finally, and we will consider more about this later, there is nothing to do but self-observe and tell the truth about the complexity and self-serving nature of mind as we witness it in ourselves and note its effects in others. Therefore, while we may be seasoned students of translational religion and prayer, we are well-advised to approach this subject of spiritual transformation cautiously, to use such labels sparingly, and to remain open and flexible to the possibility that the forms in which genuine transformation and transformational prayer may show up are likely to surprise us.

There is a tremendous temptation to look backwards, tracing one's introduction to prayer, remembering the sensations of smelling incense and gazing at the statues in the church … Stop! … and less motivation for jumping into the not-knowingness about this compelling but mysterious process. What would it be like to start from where you are, immediately? What would it be like to forget everything you have ever known about prayer and simply create an intention or make a cry to heaven; beginners all, not knowing what comes next?

II

# STARTING FROM NOWHERE

"Start from where you are" is generally good advice in any undertaking. But, like many travelers on the highway, sometimes we don't even know that—we don't know where we are and yet we are unwilling to admit it. Instead, lost as we may be, we keep driving, ashamed to ask for directions, unwilling to entertain the fact of our own inattention or ignorance. We blame the environment, the maps, anything but our own stupidity. We keep going, hoping that sooner or later we will come upon some road sign, some familiar marking. And often we do. But, often we don't. Our inattention or stubbornness can cost us many hours on the road.

In prayer, "start from where you are" can be beneficial too, although many of us don't know where we are. On one hand, we may easily misjudge our own capacities, thinking we have to go through all the stages that others have written about, mistrusting the unique workings of the spirit in our soul. On the other hand, we are strongly influenced by our projections of where we would like to be, especially if we have read one or more books on prayer. Imagination is powerful, and it is so easy to simulate the experiences of the mystics long before we are ready to embody what they have written about. We have our eyes so fixed on the future that we fail to stay simply present to the present, which is sort of a prerequisite to starting from where you are.

I would rather suggest that, where prayer is concerned, we start from nowhere. Starting from nowhere allows *anything* to happen. Without a past, without a future, with nothing, there is less likelihood that we will be seduced by self-deception. (Or maybe not. There is probably no way around self-deception completely.) The eminent Zen teacher Suzuki Roshi called this approach "beginner's mind."

On the path of prayer, beginner's mind for me implies that we enter the presence of mystery and bow down, because we are in awe at our own ignorance and our own inability to ever get things right. We let ourselves adjust to the fact that we will never be perfect "pray-ers," or accomplished holy men or women. We will always be at square one. We will, in a sense, always be awaiting our kindergarten teacher to tell us what we are going to do on this, the first day of school. We have no "where we are," we have no experience in this great Mystery School. We know nothing. And if we do know something, we gladly let go of that so the mystery may predominate.

This beginner's mind is a beneficial attitude not only in prayer but in all relationships. "Not knowing" and "knowing nothing" is a fine way to approach a marriage partner, even after thirty years. When I know nothing and am willing to embrace that, I am soft, I can be directed and helped, I can be loved. If I approach lovemaking with a notebook of techniques I may find myself missing the wondrous way in which the lover is opening himself to me this morning.

My teacher has given his devotees a form of self-inquiry that is eminently suited to the modern mind, and valuable to one who desires the next step in prayer. While Ramana Maharshi, the renowned Indian sage of the early part of the twentieth century, achieved enlightenment with the piercing question "Who am I?" my teacher encouraged us to ask, "Who am I kidding?" Typically American, he knew the psychology of those who are born into and raised with the false promises of modern advertising. We are constantly being lied to, and we are constantly lying to ourselves. People are kidding us. We are kidding ourselves. The process of spiritual life, then, is about revealing the multiple layers of the lie, the ways in which we have been deceived and have accepted and perpetuated the deception.

Who am I kidding that I know what prayer is? Maybe I do know something, or maybe I did know something the last time I addressed myself to this mystery, but right now I am naked. I am newly born. I don't yet know how to breathe in the rarefied atmosphere of this holy spirit.

Not knowing, or knowing nothing, I am suddenly free of expectations. I wait. I do not even know for what I wait. My heart is fresh. My heart is ready. Come, what may.

## Nothing to Stand On

Our prayer feels risky when it is based on not knowing. To spend a lifetime in prayer without ever getting a certificate … no Ph.D. in prayer … not even much assurance from the Dean that we're doing fine … well, it's often a bit unnerving. It's natural to want reassurance; it's natural to seek for some authority who can confirm our approach. We might suppose that our prayer was meant to build something solid, like a platform on which to stand, a place to set up house for a while, a launching pad for further exploration, or a prime spot from which to call out to God. And, maybe it will. But, we must be aware that our platform at best will be a rotating space satellite—the merest speck in infinity—and it will hang in nothing.

How do we know that our prayer is getting to the right place? Is there some cosmic ear out there somewhere, or a gigantic prayer-receiver turned in our direction? (I'm not saying there isn't!) Or is the prayer aimed inside in some way? Who shall assure us that our love, our passion, our desire for merging, our desire for service, is really not just some figment of our imagination? And, even if our spiritual guide or teacher tells us we are on the right track, will we believe him or her? Ultimately, where prayer is concerned, we can't take anyone else inside, just like we can't have an internal witness to our lovemaking. Admittedly, a lot of questions can come up when you start from nowhere. And valuable questions at that.

If we observe our worries or questions about prayer without immediately trying to fill in the blanks with answers, or without drawing conclusions that have to be acted upon, we can uncover some basic elements of our current cosmology of prayer. Having to live with our questions, without having them answered, feels dangerous—more insecure than ever.

I said to my soul, be still and wait without hope
For hope would be hope for the wrong thing; wait
    without love
For love would be love of the wrong thing; there is
    yet faith
But the faith and the love and the hope are all in
    the waiting.
Wait without thought, for you are not ready
    for thought:
So the darkness shall be the light, and the stillness
    the dancing.
                    —T. S. Eliot, from *Four Quartets*[1]

Starting from nowhere, I suggest that we take our not knowing, our standing on nothing, our imperfect prayer, our insecurity about our prayer and make *that* our prayer in the moment, recycling our doubts into our prayers, our questions into prayer, our lack of clarity into our prayer. "Lord I believe," cried out a blind man in the gospel of Jesus, "help my unbelief!"

Can we possibly allow ourselves to have no-hold on our prayer? After all, the results or the efficacy of our prayer may not be our business, if we are to believe those who have walked this path of prayer before us. Trying to determine just how effective our prayer is, or where exactly our prayer is going is more likely our attempt at some type of control. We can't have control, and shouldn't have control, in our relationship to God, as much as we'd like to. Are we going to let God be God, or, as in almost every other aspect of our lives, are we going to try to overlay our limited beliefs and expectations on the holy Other? Seems rather foolish if you ask me.

I suggest that we willingly give up our claim to a place on the faculty of the University of Prayer, and settle with gratitude to always being a "kneeler in training," as Etty Hillesum called herself.[2]

Certainly there are many valuable approaches to prayer—specific words, preferred postures, centering techniques like breath or visualization. These methods will serve us at times, especially when they are given to us by our spiritual teacher or guide. But, keep in mind that methods too may rest in a context of not-knowing, and should. When the use of any method shifts me into a context of "Now I'm getting somewhere" or "Now I'm winning," I run the risk of spiritual pride and "spiritual materialism" so well described by the Tibetan master, Chögyam Trungpa Rinpoche.[3] And with that, I've lost.

Do we really *get* somewhere in love? Good communication (and holy communion) with the other means that we're each standing on nothing, holding no past or future, losing it all, and thereby finding ourselves in love.

## A PRAYER OF NOT KNOWING

O God, I do not know how to pray. Because I do not know what it means to pray properly, to pray in such a way as to serve or worship, I must offer what I have and can do as my prayer. And here it is.

Let this posture be the prayer
Let this intention be the prayer
Let this very not-knowing be the prayer
Let this breath be the prayer
Let this resistance and discomfort be the prayer
Let this distraction be the prayer
Let this drinking of tea be the prayer
Let this eating of breakfast be the prayer
Let this hectic schedule be the prayer
Let this attempt at Remembrance be the prayer
Let the steps walked in silence across the parking lot be the prayer
Let the birdsong noted be the prayer
Let this poor journal-writing be the prayer
Let the vastness of the night sky be the prayer
Let worrying, and then dropping the worry be the prayer
Let chanting and dancing and reading be the prayer
Let dressing and undressing be the prayer
Let sleeping and rising and sleeping and rising be
    the prayer
Let missing someone be the prayer

Let memories and whispered calls for help for others be
   the prayer
Let opening the door and putting on and taking off shoes
   be the prayer
Let the keeping of simple order be the prayer
Let the celebration of light and darkness be the prayer
Let warmth and cold be the prayer
All of it, not bad, not good, just as it is and wondrous all of it
   … be the prayer
O God, in my helplessness, from nowhere, with nothing, let
   these poor prayers, as flowers, draw You to the garden
   from which their fragrance arises. Amen.

—RSR

# A Cosmology of
# Praying Dangerously

If I remember correctly, the first bit of wisdom about prayer that my teacher gave me was: "We don't pray. Only God prays, in us." He was saying essentially that prayer is something that *happens* in and through us, not something that we manipulate. Others have said it nicely too. "We *are* prayed!"

My teacher's words left me with a sigh of relief, but also somewhat troubled. After all, I'd devoted most of my life to the domain of prayer, wishing above all to become a woman of prayer—all of which kept "me" very much in the picture. Here he was wiping me out of the scene, in one sense. Despite these distressing thoughts, I also knew that he was giving me something deep and true about prayer. I knew that I would be a fool not to listen to and explore this apparent contradiction.

An existential appreciation of this mystery that "only God prays" came to me one day in a most unlikely place—in the dentist's chair. On the occasion in question, despite my best efforts, all my methods of staying centered, of praying, weren't working. With four shots of novocaine in the jaw, and a dentist and his assistant breathing over my face, cutting up my gums, yanking at my tooth, digging for nerves, wiping up saliva and blood, I was unable to keep any mental focus. In the middle of the surgery, with a mouth full of soggy gauze, I simply gave up the struggle to pray and just offered God "the whole catastrophe," as Zorba the Greek might have said ... including my defending myself against imminent pain!

Maybe it takes being pushed to a certain limit in any domain to give up the struggle in that domain, so I suppose I should have been grateful for the opportunity. At the time, however, such experiences are simply just hard, often seemingly unbearable: a parent is moaning in pain and we are helpless to alleviate it; a loved one leaves us; we get a shocking diagnosis. There is nothing inherently spiritual or transcendent about such occurrences, which may be why they are so valuable. They can't be made holy in the sense of antiseptic. They are the raw stuff of life, and sometimes there is going to be blood to prove it! In just such moments, as happened for me in that dentist's chair, the remembrance that prayer *was* going on, somewhere, by someone, was the recollection that effected a shift of consciousness for me.

In the moment when "I" couldn't pray, I knew that prayer *was* arising from the hearts of men and women and children around the world, as surely as mist was rising from meadows. I knew that my spiritual teacher was praying. I also realized that there was prayer in the coursing of my blood through my veins, in my heart beating, my lungs expanding and contracting. God simply *was*, and God was praying. I was helped (by the circumstances, or by grace) to step back and let prayer be there, through me. However it happened, prayer was taking place. There was this sense of being instructed in simply giving up and being advised to, "Let Me do it. Let Me carry you through prayer. Let Me pray through you." The "Me" being ... well, the Divine, God, my teacher; all of the above, perhaps.

The related gift of that gruesome morning for me was another take on this process of transformation. This time, it was about the transformation of suffering into prayer. As the surgery progressed, I was thinking about the idea of not wasting the discomfort in my mouth and the fear and expectations of pain in my mind, wishing to make use of this pain in a way that could be of service to others. But, I didn't know *how* to do that. Despite the fact that I'd long ago developed the habit of saying to God, "Take this and use it for the highest purposes," formulating intention in all sorts of circumstances, today the appreciation that such a transformation was possible merely through intention was tangible. I suppose I was amenable to receiving something in that moment, because I *really* wanted it—this leap from self-involvement in pain to useful prayer. So, with the dentist's drill vibrating the roots of my teeth, sending shivers up my spine and causing me to grip the arms of the chair, I swallowed a big slice of the wonder and mystery of prayer. I recognized that the transformation I was asking for may always remain unknowable at some levels, and I embraced the *not knowing*. At the same time, a faith arose in me that God does know how to effect such transformation, and could and would and *was* doing it in and with and through me. Put another way, I could allow the Holy Spirit, or Christ, or the Buddha or my guru, to pray in me, transforming the gross substance of my pain and fear into the sublime substance of prayer and praise.

Others have recorded similar stories about their experiences, aware that Christ was coexistent with their body, and that Christ was bearing their pain, transforming that pain into prayer. They too didn't have to do anything, as it was already done in and through them.

Corrie Ten Boom, in her book *The Hiding Place*, tells a story that verifies this point further. After the war, following her confinement at Ravensbrück by the Nazis, where she suffered humiliation and extremes of deprivation, she traveled in

Germany speaking on the subject of forgiveness. In a church service in Munich she was shocked for the first time to recognize among the congregation a former S.S. man, one of her actual jailers.

Meeting her as the church was emptying, the man expressed his gratitude for her message, and put out his hand to her. But Corrie was as if paralyzed, unable to forgive him, unable to extend her hand. Feelings of anger and vengeance arose in her, and she immediately saw the horror of them. "Lord Jesus," she prayed, "forgive me and help me to forgive him." Several times she tried to raise her hand back, tried to smile, but could not. Again she prayed, asking for God's own forgiveness to heal her.

When at last she was able to take his hand a "most incredible thing happened."

> From my shoulder along my arm and through my hand a current seemed to pass from me to him, while into my heart sprang a love for this stranger that almost overwhelmed me.
>
> And so I discovered that it is not on our forgiveness any more than on our goodness that the world's healing hinges, but on His. When He tells to love our enemies, He gives, along with the command, the love itself.[1]

Thank goodness that we don't have to mind God's business. We don't have to know the technology of prayer, nor do we have to carry the responsibility for *how* it happens. In fact, it may be best that we don't know. Embracing the not-knowingness is a great blessing.

As I sat in the dentist's chair that day, what I *could* mind was the reality that here, amidst the yankings and the grindings and the saliva dribbling, my heart desired to extend itself.

I longed to give this energy over, into something larger, to offer with conscious attention and intention this raw stuff of being human for the relief of the sufferings of others.

Could I understand this logically? No. But it was beneficial to simply rest in the awareness that "only God prays," and to watch where that took me.


## ALWAYS ALREADY PRAYING

Prayer is "… breathing in and breathing out the one breath of the Universe."          —Hildegard of Bingen

We pray and we hunger for prayer because prayer *is* the most basic relationship that life has with life. All life, by the fact that it *is* life, is in constant communication and communion with itself. Trees are in communication with the wind, their leaves in communion with the sap in their branches. Animals communicate with other animals—hearts beating, lungs expanding, blood coursing, eyes scanning the horizon—sometimes moving together, sometimes apart. At the subatomic level, electrons bump into electrons, and this communication effects chemical and nuclear reactions. At the heart of the heart of the human being throbs the life force, utterly mysterious and yet somehow knowable. The mystics and poets say, "God praises God," and this praise of God for God drives all things forward. The ocean constantly ebbs and flows its praise upon the ocean. The breath of man or woman, rising and falling, moment to moment, year in and year out, is visible witness of the organic prayer of creation. Attached as we are to the source of all, we cannot be dis-attached and live. We live in the relationship that is prayer.

To say "we pray" is actually like saying, "we live." But, it is a helpful statement nonetheless. Some of us don't realize how precious life is. Some of us take our prayer for granted, or think we don't know how to pray.

Prayer is falling into, or stepping into, or resting in, resonance with the force that drives creation. As such, prayer is always happening, and is nothing less than the expression of our true nature. Prayer is the orientation of the human heart, body, emotions and mind toward communication and communion with God. And, since the basic truth of our non-separation from God means that we are always "in God" anyway, prayer is the expression of the truth of our relatedness to God.

Recently, I read one man's take on prayer. He said that if you examine the motivation for prayer you will find insecurity and the need to reach out for some protection, some salvation. His conclusion: he'd rather not lower himself to such gross, base activities. I thought to myself what a fool he was. Does he also not eat because eating is based in survival needs? Does he deny himself attraction to a woman because it might excite his lust? Was there no place to be a beginner in his approach to prayer, allowing that there may be a wisdom that was simply expressing itself in immature terms in the beginning stages?

We all know that much prayer comes out of our fear, our insecurity, our necessity, our selfishness. But, when a mother or father holds a newborn and gazes at it, the mood of that is *not* insecurity but awe. The mood is love and gratitude, and wonder. The feelings are actually often so deep as to be beyond expression. In those moments of gazing, nothing is happening except for love and sweet communion. This communion is what we are genuinely hungry for, and this hunger draws us to pray.

We have all tasted or intuited this lack of separation from God as a foundational reality, if only for the briefest moment. Our reaching out in prayer, then, may simply be the cry of the heart for that reality to be expressed in and through us in all ways, at all times. When we stand in awe at the mystery of God's already-present union with us, when we are in "radical amazement" at life, as Rabbi Abraham J. Heschel would say, or when "our eyes are opened to that surprise character of the world around us," as Brother David Steindl-Rast has written, we are praying.[2] Actually, we are involved in adoration, which I think is the highest calling of the human soul. Without adoration in relationship to life, we are dull and dry and desperate. To genuinely adore is to pray dangerously.

To pray dangerously is not to adopt a new method, however. Praying dangerously is actually a context, or a framework, on which or within which almost any method of prayer can be placed. When the contextual basis of our prayer is that of surrender to the will of God, then our prayer can take any number of forms. Even if we are petitioning the Divine, which may at times be an indicator of a misdirected context, we can still be praying to the heart of the matter. Jesus in the Garden of Gethsemane, on the night before his crucifixion implored, "Let this chalice pass from me ..." but then added the great words of love and the most dangerous prayer, "nevertheless not my will, but Thine be done."

The cosmology of dangerous prayer is not difficult, it is based in the foundational understanding that we already are that which we seek. Our prayer is our means of awakening ourselves to what has always been the one reality. We are already ... well, you name it: good, perfect, enlightened, beloved, saved, not separate from God, the son or daughter of God, the vessel of the Buddha nature, the lover to the Beloved ... the list goes on and on. The Hindu scriptures express it beautiful-ly: *Poornaat poorna-mudachyate* ... "From the Perfect springs the Perfect. If the Perfect is taken from the Perfect, only the Perfect remains." Or, in the central Vedic maxim, *Tat Tvat Asi*, "Thou are That."

This context of perfection is the context we seek to recall and rest in. We long for this true home. We want to inhabit it, and to enliven it in our cells. Such a context is nothing we have to establish, because it already is, but we do have to remember it, and that generally takes effort because we've worked so hard to deny it.

The illusion that we are other than "That" is thick and deep, and the illusion that we must do something radical, terrible, wrenching, to merit our birthright is also an illusion. Thomas Merton speaks of the seeker who casts himself as Prometheus, needing to steal fire from the gods. This view of the Divine as some master deceiver who hides the treasure of itself and must have the treasure stolen, who makes the path difficult in order to thwart the lives of poor humans, is Prometheus's dilemma. This view of the Divine is misguided, but pervasive nonetheless. It is especially difficult to overcome since the other side of the paradox of "already Perfect" is that usually we *do* have to struggle, and sometimes with extraor-dinary measures, because our habit of denying our birthright has become so ingrained.

Habit and misguided thinking do not easily surrender their dominance. Therefore, some of our prayer-work will rightly be a means to soften our defenses against the One who pursues us with love.

The desire that we have for prayer, even if we can't verbalize why we want it, or what prayer is, or what God is, is indicative that prayer is already alive in us. Such desire, as indistinct as it may be, is itself the longing of the One for union with itself, the hunger of Divinity to claim full possession of its own. It is God calling out to God.

## FOOD FOR GOD

"Become a tasty morsel for the Divine," my teacher told me.

Long before I realized the implications of the statement, I loved the feel of it. He was alluding to an underlying principle of the universe that "everything is food for everything else."[3] That is, we feed from life forms in the food chain below us, and higher entities feed from us. Such a statement describes the process of spiritual *sadhana* (spiritual work) as well: You work on self. You refine your life. You open yourself to the benediction of God—becoming filled with a radiance, a juiciness, an aroma that is attractive. Some of that attraction is noted by the people in your environment. Kids, like flies, start giving you the wink. Even if you aren't pretty or shapely, there is that certain something that alerts others of your richness. They can feed from you, so to speak. And they will. Attractive people of all types (those with physical attractiveness and those with spiritual radiance) are subject to attacks from energy vampires who try to feed off the life force that these attractive others possess.

The Divine, God, or beings of more subtle substance are similarly attracted by richness. God is fed on the radiance of creation, on whatever serves Its purposes, and on the foods that creation produces. To take our analogy further, when the Divine smells a reliable source of purified, useable food, It will steadily come to call. It will regularly feed upon Itself, in this case on the man or woman whose radiant energy has turned himself or herself into a tasty morsel.

We serve the Divine as transformers of the material substance of food, water, air and impressions into the sacred substances of praise, adoration and gratitude. Our prayer is food for God. We also feed *from* the Divine as we pray, in much the same way that energy is exchanged in a kiss.

We use this term "soul food" quite loosely these days, but the esoteric meaning of the words is quite profound. What we are really saying is that food not only carries a nutritive value that nourishes the body, supplying the vitamins and minerals and phytochemicals necessary to maintain equilibrium. It carries other nutrients that feed more subtle organs and maintain balance in those systems that can't be tested in the lab. When Mom prepares that favorite dish for her child's birthday she is giving her love along with the noodles and sauce. Her family feels cared for. Food also carries the qualities or *rasa* (mood) of sensuality. It carries a power that says "you are fortified," in all kinds of ways.

The soul is fed just as the body is fed, but not with gross substance. Rather, the soul eats and is nourished by the love that went into the food and the atmosphere in which the food is served—namely the impressions of an environment. When these are pure and abundant the soul is sustained; when they are dark and stark they will either poison or dull the soul, or they will require a type of transformation in order for the soul to be able to use them.

We don't live in a bright world all the time. A healthy soul knows how to roll with the punches. It knows how to make lemonade from the bruised fruit of the world's situations. One who is trained in the science and art of transformation knows how to place themselves in the midst of hell and to turn negativity into energy, into the substance of food. Let's take a concrete example. We all feel anger. We can be swept into the anger and thus spiral down into a puddle of depression and discontent. Anger is hot energy. It therefore has much potential for usable substance. If anger is allowed to simply be present without the necessity for negative expression; if anger is breathed; if the subtle energy of anger is allowed to rush through the body without the need to do anything about it, it can become energy for work, rather than energy for destruction.

This is the meaning of *tantra*—despite numerous misinterpretations in this day and age. Tantra is the non-rejection of all things, not the indulgence in all things. With a tantric relationship to life we are attuned to the energetic substance that can be extracted from every situation. We are aware that food for God can be grown anywhere, at any time.

Time set aside for prayer, or any form of remembrance or attention to prayer throughout the day, is an opportunity for the soul to feed from and grow the substance that infuses all life, and is always available. We can call it the substance of God, or divine grace, or basic goodness (as Tibetan master Chögyam Trungpa Rinpoche has named it), or *prana*, or life force.

We pray, or rather we are "in prayer" as in a working laboratory. We are alchemitizing the circumstances of ordinary life into a substance usable by ourselves and the Divine.

We are consumed. We consume. Prayer is a feast of feeding.

## WHAT PRAYER IS NOT

Recently I picked up a book about the mystical life. Since the author was a minister and a theologian I assumed she would stretch my views about prayer. Yet, as I opened to the designated chapter on prayer I was surprised with an essay about how she had prayed for a trip to Israel and after many years her prayer had been answered. She wrote from her hotel room in Damascus.

Like the author of the book in question, I am aware that focused intention seems to be one of the most powerful tools the human mind possesses. Apparently, and I'm completely convinced of this, such intentionality is what brings one's dreams into reality. It should not be dismissed. However, major league football players win games with this kind of intention, and some probably have no prayer in mind. I'm therefore asking for some clarified distinctions here, similar to the distinction about translational and transformational religion drawn earlier.

Focusing intention in asking for something—whether that something be a trip to Israel or healing from cancer—is *unquestionably* effective. I know because I've done it. I've made intentions to the universe—spoken them to the night sky, written them on big sheets of cardboard which I decorated as collages, made them into magnetized signs and posted them on my refrigerator door. I've asked the students in my college courses to do the same. I've told them that intention seems to be an unmatched vehicle for manifesting the impossible, even though I don't pretend to know precisely how the process works.

One year I wanted to go to Europe with a group of friends. The trip would cost $4000, total. I had no expendable income at the time. Instead, I made the intention. I said out loud, and to a few companions, "I don't know how I'm going to afford it, but I'm going." Then I signed up for the trip, assuming that the money would follow. After two weeks I got a call from my co-author on our first book. Would I like to undertake a fast project with him? He was sure we could get a cash advance from a publisher. Yes, I said, and set to work.

Three weeks later the contract arrived from the publisher. My advance? Four thousand dollars, exactly! I'm not kidding. These stories are a dime a dozen.

I think we need to keep this kind of petitioning and manifesting within the domain in which it is born, raised, and put to practice. Let's keep it within the definition of the mind's power to focus and thereby catalyze itself, or others, thereby setting in motion a heightened sensitivity to possibility. Let's keep it in the domain of all things being connected, energetically, in a vast interdependent matrix of life; that is, nothing moves in my world but it does not affect the movement of the stars, and vice versa.

But, let's cautiously approach equating our "power of positive thinking" efforts with the type of dangerous prayer I'm suggesting here, unless, of course, we can *really* surrender, fully, as Christ did in the Garden of Gethsemane, to receiving God's will *regardless* of one's own opinions. As we have noted before, Christ was in great anguish about the approach of his excruciating death, and cried out, "Father, if it be possible, let this chalice pass from me." But, recall that he ended that prayer with, "Nevertheless, not my will, but Thine be done." Be honest, how many of us can truly do that?

If such affirming and intention-setting is meant to bring us to the point of surrendering our will completely to God's will—let's have more of it. But let's also carefully examine if we are doing what Elisabeth Kübler-Ross called "bargaining," her word for one of the stages of grief: "Oh God, if you only grant me a reprieve this time, I promise I'll never drink again." Or, "Heal me this time, Lord, and I'll go to church every day … " or whatever.

Also, such "prayer" can run the risk of serving as proof that "our" prayers are more effective, or stronger than other peoples' prayers. After all, there are lots of people praying to win that game, or get that job! We might start to fear that unless we are "getting the goods" that God is somehow not listening. Faith indicates that prayer is answered in ways that are mysterious. After all, I recall that Jesus said to his disciple Thomas, "Blessed are they who have not seen, and yet have believed."

Heartbreak and failure in the short run may be the ways in which we come to know that only Love endures. So, while it is psychologically healthy to have strong intentions, and often provokes additional inspiration, I'm not ready to call this technology "transformational prayer." What about you? For our purposes, let's consider that much of translational prayer is about me talking to God or to myself, attempting to ready myself for battle. Let's say that transformational prayer has no "me" in it. That's not easy.

Many imploring prayers or petitionary prayers are actually acts of faith, of praise, or of worship. To call upon God to "open my eyes" or to cry out "Lord, have mercy" is not like asking God to buy you a Mercedes Benz, or praying to survive a plane crash. Rather, such faith-filled prayers are acknowledgements of relationship with the Divine and invitations to a deeper relationship. We want our eyes open so that we may see God more clearly in order to live in, as and through God. We pray for mercy, not because God is condemning us and we are begging for reprieve. Instead, we lay our pain and our sin at God's feet, admitting to ourselves and before all creation that we are helpless without alignment to the Divine Principle; that we are hopeless when we forget and deny our inseparable connection to God. We pray "Lord, have mercy" because we have missed the mark once again; we have caused harm to ourselves and others, and it is only right and just that we admit it as a prelude to recommitting to love.

Unless we are ready to seriously question our approach to prayer we cannot enter the domain of the unknown, the unknowing and the emptiness out of which truth, unadorned, unattached, unsentimental can arise. Let's start from here. I believe we are up for it.

## RADICAL RELIANCE ON GOD

My guru died a few months before this edition of *Praying Dangerously* went to press. Lee Lozowick, who first suggested that I write about prayer in 2001, and whose inspiration for radical prayer fill the pages of this book, left his physical body on November 16, 2010, two days before his sixty-seventh birthday. While he had been living as passionately as ever, and with cancer for three years, his death still came as a shock, and our little community of devotees, some of whom were with him for thirty-five years (I was for twenty-six) both celebrated and mourned his transition. We also turned to greater love and caring for one another.

Lee demonstrated a life of radical reliance on God, the subtitle of this book, which is why I can write about this subject with some strong reference point. When he burst onto the American spiritual scene in 1975 he offered a genuine alternative to what Chögyam Trungpa Rinpoche has called the "myth of freedom" under which contemporary seekers were laboring. His was not a new message, but it was a unique, controversial and extraordinarily skillful presentation at the time. To the hippies of the '70s, heading to India and some fast bliss path to enlightenment, he proposed "spiritual slavery" as the way to fly. To be a "spiritual slave" literally meant that one was ready and willing to put all one's eggs in one basket—God's basket, not one's own. A spiritual slave was one who had seen through the illusions of freedom of choice and had opted for the will of the Powers that Be, willingly squandering his or her precious life for a purpose.

What spiritual slavery and radical reliance are about is a fiery love—a love so strong that the pray-er *wants* no diversions, no extraneous freedoms or choices. She or he only wants Mary's place at the feet of Jesus. He or she wants Rumi's uncompromising devotion to the Beloved, his Shams. No choice but Love; no choice but God alone. In that choice for no choice, he or she accepts a willing slavery, wasted for an aim greater than they could ever fulfill in a lifetime, but happy in their bonded service.

To rely upon God for all the details of one's life, for all the places and things that will absorb one's attention, and perhaps even to the degree of reliance for food, clothing, shelter ... well, that's radical! Who among us can *do* it? And that's the clear point: we can't "do" this. Radical reliance of this type is a grace—the grace of surrender. "We" can't accomplish such a transformation, but God can. And our prayer can state our willingness to be so used, if we wish it. Holding this as possibility, we can be inspired to let go in small ways; we can turn over the day to God's work, God's service, and then pay attention each time we find ourselves taking back our gift. That's how our intention is earned.

Still, there are contemporary examples of individuals who *were* thrown completely on the mercy of the tides, and were (or still are) carried by a current that supports what ultimately serves. My guru Lee Lozowick was one of those rare persons. A Christian hermit monk, Abba Jonathan of God, a friend who lives in the Arizona desert, exemplifies the same. Yogi Ramsuratkumar, my guru's guru, was a beggar who lived on the streets of south India, fully surrendered to God's direction, and his life was one of listening, attuned to the direction of "my Father," as he affectionately called the Ultimate. Catherine Doherty, whose work with the poor and in establishing bastions of contemplative prayer in the U.S., Canada and around the world, was graced to follow the injunction of the scriptures: "Go sell what you have and give it to the poor and come follow me," was such a slave. Her rich and abundant life was handled by reliance on the Holy Spirit down to the smallest detail.

## A Dangerous Path

In 1980, at an ashram in Pune, India, I experienced the thrill of God's invitation to surrender. Drunk with bliss, I called home to tell my husband that I was staying on in India, indefinitely. He was upset. I didn't care. I was "captured" by something bigger than me, and that was all that mattered. I told him to sell my expensive bicycle, sell whatever I had of value and to send me the money. He wouldn't do it. I was angry. I called a wealthy friend and asked for support, and was rewarded for my efforts. I changed my plane ticket and signed on for more bliss. Three weeks later I contracted hepatitis. My self-directed bliss journey now became a quest for adequate daily food, rest, medical assistance and much needed companionship. Alone, I spent the next four months in bed, barely able to move to the bathroom.

Such casualties of intoxication were not uncommon in the field of energy I played in there. I recall seeing a young Western man sitting outside the ashram gates, in dirty clothes, sores on his legs and feet, begging for money to get back to the states. He had torn up his plane ticket and passport in a fit of spiritual enthusiasm. When the high faded, as it always does, he had used his last funds to keep his bliss alive by smoking a lot of ganja. I observed that other pilgrims, especially those newly arrived from the West, kept a wide berth from this obviously desperate soul.

I paid a heavy price for my own incident of blissful naiveté. As I look back on this painful period, still always grateful for the lesson, I see that while surrender was my desire, I was self-centered and immature in my appreciation of this path. Certainly I wanted to surrender, but I wanted it essentially to create freedom from suffering (more bliss) for me. I was determined to "do it my way," regardless of the pain it might cause others.

A life of prayer, including a radical reliance on God, requires a foundation of maturity. And no one earns maturity without making a lot of mistakes. As we put in our time on the path, if our intention remains clear, we face the painful truth of our own self-obsession over and over. We must then bear this pain, often in great remorse, without letting it crush us. Self-observation without judgment is the only way to grow up.

There is no substitute for experienced guidance and the support of mature friends in our prayer life. But the caveat always is that we need to trust others, and like me in 1980, many of us won't abide the advice of those who could genuinely help us. Fools do rush in where angels fear to tread, and blessedly God takes care of even fools, as long as they keep renewing intention and attempting to learn from their mistakes.

Especially where radical moves are concerned, my guru always taught me that *we* don't have to worry about the big and significant changes in life, as *they will make us*! Had I availed myself of this wisdom at the time that I opted to cast all caution aside, I would have realized that surrender was God's business, not mine. I would have trusted that if and when surrender was to happen, the environment of India was certainly not a pre-requisite to it. And *that* would have been a vote in favor of radical reliance or spiritual slavery.

## LISTENING FOR GOD

For most of us, radical reliance on God will not be about physical poverty. We probably won't ride our bicycles across North America with a sign bearing a scriptural reference, although I once met a sixty-five-year-old woman at a McDonald's along Interstate 80 in Nebraska who was doing just that. Our expressions of radical prayer and reliance on God will more likely be about listening. While we often think of prayer and surrender as something we *do*, it is actually more about non-doing, allowing and awaiting. To live radically surrendered to or reliant on God, we would pay close attention, watch the signs, and listen clearly.

Life in the domain of listening for God is a moment to moment affair in the here and now. I can't listen for God in the past. I can't listen to, or surrender to or love God in the future. I only have this moment in which to love God. When I spoke these words to a group of friends recently, one woman let out a huge sigh of relief. "Wow," she said, "that makes life so manageable." The rest of us agreed. It also actually makes life interesting and even magical. Moment to moment we listen—which for me means that I take a step back from attempting to control what is. Rather than asserting my will, I relax my grip, develop a wide-ranging field attention, and look at and listen to what is in the environment that needs my focus. Ultimately, I allow love to direct the course of things. I know this sounds a bit vague, but I think you've had the experience many times. If you've ever cared for children you know what it feels like to simply go with their flow, allowing them to direct the play rather than trying to steer them into a game or activity of your choice.

I had the privilege of traveling with my spiritual teacher on many occasions, in different parts of the world. Once, as we followed him through a series of markets in southern France, a friend and I left the group to do some lightning-quick grocery shopping. When we returned to the van, Lee asked us about our purchases. When we told him that we had bought salad veggies for the next three days he shook his head sadly. "Never trust in tomorrow when you can stock up with more than you need today," or words closely to that effect, he said with sarcasm dripping. Our fear that we would not have enough had caused us to over buy, and to run the risk of having food spoil before it was used. Lee, on the other hand, was an advocate of the spontaneity that might delight everyone when necessity presented itself. He was always being thwarted, he told us, because of our over planning. When we arrived at our day's destination he liked nothing better than to create a meal with whatever was at hand. If we had little, he might create a salad of all the leftovers in the refrigerator, after which we'd drink tea and eat the chocolates that people often gave him. Or, he might suggest that we all go out for a gourmet meal. But, our well-meaning efforts at control, based in survival, so easily undermined the magic he hoped to enact with us. *Ah well.*

And so, as I sat at my desk at 3:30 PM on a Sunday afternoon writing this essay, I realized that this moment I had the opportunity to pray. I stopped, turning toward remembrance.

Coincidently, before I could finish typing the previous sentence my husband was at the door, asking almost apologetically if I could spare him a few minutes to help move a table. When I read to him what I'd just written about listening for God, we both smiled, and I was on my feet immediately, and with gratitude. For me, that's just one tiny example of the way God speaks.

## THE SACRAMENT OF THE PRESENT MOMENT

*The Sacrament of the Present Moment* is also the title of a book by a French Jesuit, written over three-hundred years ago. This foundational spiritual text is the work of Jean-Pierre de Caussade, who also authored the classic *Abandonment to Divine Providence*. In my understanding, a sacrament is a sign of grace, a sign of the sacred, and each moment is such a sacrament, such a potential. Thus we have constant signposts pointing the way to living in communion with God. A theology of this type is not dry, rigid or doctrinaire. Rather, this French priest encourages his readers to a joyous, affirming, and ultimately selfless abandonment to God. Through authentic contemplation, along with facing ourselves honestly and openly, the comfort and fulfillment of a life suffused with grace are revealed to us.

For our purposes, let's convert this phrase into a verb and consider how we might "sacramentalize every moment." What if we were to *choose*—not because it were proven one way or the other—to simply find God's Hand or God's Face in every situation of life? What if we were to look for gift and grace in every person we met, every circumstance that presented itself? What if every gap in the busyness of life became an invitation to enter the sanctuary of the inner temple? What if, down to this very breath, we contextualized everything as holy?

In my experience, regardless of the logic of this approach, my life flowers when I make these choices to sacramentalize the moment. Life contracts and dries up when I let emotional reactivity or doctrine or a belief system regarding a person or situation determine my view. Life works when I am radically relying upon God, radically attached to something beyond my own small definition of self. Such finding of or listening for God's direction, awaiting God's design, makes me receptive to whatever presents itself, be it prayer, service and the expression of compassion, or immersion in chaos, confusion and breakdown.

In form, to practice the sacramentalizing of the present moment one lives a big YES. In this moment, I say yes and turn to Love. In this moment next, I say yes and turn to Love. Does that sound easy? Well, how about in this moment? Choose!

I gain great courage in this practice from the words of my teacher:

> What I am suggesting is that God knows full well our exact state and will provide all the resources needed, in the proper time and place, given our exact capacities and abilities in the moment, for our continued drawing nearer to Him, in our ongoing revelation of already present Union or Perfection as "what is, as it is, here and now." If we simply intend to serve or to know Him and live the lives He has given us ... He will chart our paths and direct our activities, establishing us as we need to be established in order to optimally and most effectively service Him, which is no different from optimally and most effectively serving the whole of His creation, in the forms directly in front of us here and now.[4]

To rest in this mood is to pray dangerously.

IV

# IGNITING THE INNER LIFE

Only those with an inner life are capable of finding, and then following through with, their destiny. All the rest are merely "food for the moon" as the Russian mystic and teacher George Gurdjieff would say. By "food for the moon" he meant a type of useful fertilizer, but nothing that effected the forward evolution of humanity.[1] So much of contemporary culture is utterly soul-less, and millions of people in the midst of infinite diversions, comforts and distractions suffer lives of quiet desperation. Their inner lives are dormant. At best, spiritual and metaphysical fads from feng-shui to tantric sex may strike a match in this dark wilderness. But, more likely, such activities merely afford more sophisticated, and therefore deadly, consolation to people who otherwise have no destiny, no inner life. Suggestions for how to spiritualize daily life are innumerable—there are scores of books on the market today that detail these. To do little rituals around one's flower garden is one thing, to offer one's life in the process of transformation from self-obsession to God-life, or truth, or for the liberation of others, is quite another.

Inner life is synonymous with inner being. We have such being when we are attuned with and moved by Being itself, and consciously participate in Being's unfolding. Rather than finding ourselves at the effect of whatever prevailing winds are blowing—whether these be the insane patterns of identification created by our own mind, including all our addictions and cravings, or the latest fashion craze or political movement—the one in possession of inner being maintains attention on his or her intentional purpose. The man or woman with inner being is more likely to remain present to the here and now, which seems to be the only place where Being, or God, lives. Such a person is connected with themselves, mindful and intentional in thought, speech and action. Whatever helps in the building of being, or presence, or awareness, or genuine compassion, therefore, builds the inner life. Prayer, meditation or contemplation, because it stops us short in our endless whirling around for fascinating alternatives, is a foundation of the temple of being.

The analogy of the building of an interior temple, a temple of the heart, as a house for the Divine is a useful description of the work involved in creating the inner life, a living spiritual life. If the foundation is shallow or the building materials are shabby, the whole superstructure is constantly in jeopardy, no matter how grand it may appear to the untrained eye. Our temple will be as strong, as elegant and as attractive to the Deity as our prayer is constant and steeped in both humility and longing. It will be a sanctuary to ourselves and to others, insofar as we know our own minds and are able to recognize the illusions and attachments that disrupt the inner silence. The temple will be pure, in the sense of integral, as we are true to our own word, practicing a type of inner listening that keeps us both flexible and disciplined. It will be luminous, lit from within by the flames of gratitude for the miracle of just what is. Our temple will be a living invocation of Divinity, a beacon that spans the heavens, inviting God to merge with humanity to the degree that we honor and even celebrate the body that houses it. And these are but a few of many ways of building the inner life, a few of the many ways of praying dangerously.

## CONSTANCY BY INTENTION

A prayer life is no different from a genuine love life. Once the infatuation stage of any romance begins to fade, as the hormones level out, the couple is faced with a crucial moment of decision. Will they take on the work of relationship, moving themselves from the euphoric hills to the heights of the mountain, or will they end their picnic foray and try again with another partner? Unfortunately, as the divorce rates testify, many lack the stamina, education or skill to build love—a love that transforms the hearts of its participants. Even if they don't divorce, many others settle for a life of tolerance for the sake of security, at best.

Influenced as we are by such a culture of inconstancy, will we then have what it takes to develop constancy in our prayer life? Certainly we are drawn to prayer. We are attracted to the people who embody prayer. We try prayer, and we like it. We are infatuated. For a period of time we are carried on the waves of grace that are always available to one who sets an intention. And, when the waves happen to roll us up on a deserted shore, or when the sea moves into doldrums, do we have what it takes to not abandon our trust? Or, will we whip out our cell-phones as quickly as we can say, "This is not what I bargained for," and call for a helicopter?

Step number one in building a life of prayer is recognizing that all experiences, especially the warm and cuddly ones that we have associated with prayer, are going to pass away. Prayer is not about accumulating experiences, no matter how blissful or illuminating. A genuine prayer life is not a life free from pain, terror, discomfort, insecurity or doubt. In fact, to open ourselves to the forces of life *as it is* is actually to invite pain—a pain that we willingly share with others, a pain we can use as fuel for our prayer. My teacher is fond of saying that, "Enlightenment is the knowledge that all experience is transitory, including enlightenment." All experience in prayer is transitory. But, will we abandon prayer because of that? Or, will we travel across the desert despite the heat, drawn forward in faith because we know that this is the path that must be navigated because this is not other than life as it is— sometimes bliss-filled, sometimes full of hot sand?

When the honeymoon is over, we build constancy or reliability in prayer like we build love, by both intention and by practice. Some of us take a long time to exhaust our testing and pushing-away strategies toward the other, convinced that they couldn't possibly love us. When, despite the odds, they hang in there with us through thick or thin, some of us actually learn to trust, opening ourselves to love. Such constancy is also enormously attractive to the Divine, Who, it seems, is always looking for good instruments for the accomplishment of Its purposes.

Intention or the refinement of purpose is one of the strongest energies in the universe. It is what distinguishes the human from the dollop of sea foam. Our intention to pray, regardless of how we think or how we feel at any moment, coupled with our putting ourselves "on the mat" as they say in the martial arts (or on the meditation cushion, or in the chair, or on our knees before the altar … the forms are numerous) sets in place the cornerstone of our inner temple. Intention and practice determine the direction in which one is facing— whether we face illusion or reality. The intention to pray, in the way we speak of it here, is an orientation toward the real. Such an intention, affirmed day to day, moment to moment, and stabilized in practice, will announce our willingness to be shown the insubstantiality of all phenomena. No wonder such clear and powerful witness invites God's help. It bespeaks trustworthiness, receptivity and possibility.

The power of our intention is the key to praying always, which is the injunction of many great spiritual traditions, and something that many of us would like to implement into our daily lives. Such constant prayer requires great discipline of mind. It requires the guidance of a teacher to refine. But, we can, no matter what stage of practice we are at, take a moment or two at the beginning of the day and another few moments at the beginning of new activities throughout our day to re-member what we're all about, what we want of our lives, and to offer the work of our hands, our mind, our heart to the Divine Alchemist who transforms gross substance into gold. We can turn everything back to God all day long.

Our intention turns an unconscious life into a life of prayer, and even a weak intention is a good beginning. We generally begin to pray with self-serving intention—because we are suf-fering and want relief, or because we are confused and want answers, or because we are frightened and want comfort. If we waited until our intention was totally pure and altruistic we would never pray. Our initial intention gets us to the altar or the meditation cushion. Over time, our intention evolves and our practice becomes a positive addiction. Subtly, and sometimes imperceptibly, a shift takes place in the context of our prayer. We didn't start out there, perhaps, but we may find ourselves praying as an expression of our gratitude, or out of our deep desire to serve humanity, or for a reason we can't even imagine now. And that makes all the difference. Our prayer somehow starts to invoke God, and over time leads to relationship with God. Finally, God becomes a reliable ally. Or to say it another way, we come to trust God in all the circumstances in our lives. Such trust is not just plucked from thin air. Our trust arises because we've invoked and built relationship by intention.

## TIME, PLACE AND METHOD

I am in favor of prayer, period. Even clumsy prayer, immature prayer, manipulative prayer—as poor a reflection of what God is as that may be—is an attempt to bring God into the equation, and I'm all for that. We all have to start out from wherever we are, or from nowhere.

But, to build a life of prayer, that requires a bit more attention and intention; a bit of maturing. We build a life of prayer by steps and stages. We create a time, a place and a method, and then we follow through with what we have set up ... yes, we follow through. And when we don't follow through in this moment, we start over in the next moment. We follow through again.

That phrase "time, place and method" is a perfect one to apply to prayer. It originated as a means of determining whether a person who talks about or thinks about suicide is actually a likely candidate. Most people at some point in their lives have fleeting desires for dissolution as a solution to their pain. But few will plan out their self-destruction to the point of gathering the equipment, establishing the time, and determining the place at which they will do the deed—thus, "a time, a place and a method." As crisis counselors know, when someone gets to that point the situation has moved to the red-alert stage. It is time for serious intervention.

A transformational prayer life is a suicide to ego. The one who begins this journey of prayer will not be the one who ends it. Therefore, if we are serious about accomplishing this death to self we must also get our act together and make it happen, rather than merely talk about it with well-meaning but ineffective, uncommitted people. "Oh, are you in a prayer group? I've often thought about joining one myself ... "

The time, the place and the method may be determined and supported by a group gathering or a functional ritual—like attending a prayer circle every Saturday, or Mass and communion service every Sunday, or group sitting practice on Wednesday nights. But, a life of prayer requires that what is tasted in these opportunities becomes a part of every day. We need more than a weekly suicide. We need a daily death to self; ideally we need to die as often as possible throughout the day.

Tired excuses about not having enough time to cultivate a life of prayer don't cut it. Every book on the market that deals with prayer will offer you a myriad of suggestions for how to find the time for prayer, or how to steal the time, which is more to the point. Instead of belaboring the obvious once again, let's enter into this consideration through the back door. Let's recall that despite the fact that most of us live more or less from the context or mindset that love is scarce, that context is not a true one. Let's affirm that scarcity of love is an illusion, albeit an illusion that we agree to believe, and then suffer. Nevertheless, love is not scarce. And when we love something, really love it, we make time for it. We find time for it, even if that means cutting down on sleep, or skipping TV altogether, or (God forbid!) lowering our standards of perfection in some domain and reorienting our priorities. The more we reinforce the notion that time or anything else is scarce by endlessly whining about it, the more we will believe ourselves to be impotent and uncreative in effecting change. We are not impotent. We are brilliantly creative. We will have the time when we are willing to make prayer a priority.

The only aspect of time for prayer that bears consideration in a book about praying dangerously is that of experimenting with the length of time we devote to prayer at any one session, and the time or times of day that seem to optimize our prayer. After all, we are explorers in this realm of the heart, the realm of consciousness. We will want to learn what serves our intention and what diminishes it.

The science fiction writers are onto something when they describe the concept of "windows in time" or gateways in the matrix—points of access between dimensions of reality. Prayer is such an access. Call the different dimensions whatever you wish, I'll call them the domain of self-obsession in contrast to the domain of God-life. Prayer for me is the substance, the process, the map or the formula whereby I move from self-obsession to communion with God. My question becomes, "What are the circumstances that best enhance the possibility of catching the 'window in time,' and what are the situations and circumstances that discourage such possibility?" I have learned that certain times of the day and night are more conducive to access of another domain. Perhaps, for whatever reason, my defenses are less adamant at these times, and I am more flexible of soul and perception. These times lend themselves to moving into God remembrance rather than staying stuck in self-obsession.

According to some cultures and cosmologies, like that of the Native American and the Yogic, the "veils between the worlds" are supposedly thinner at certain times of day—at sunrise and sunset, for instance, or at first light, which may be much earlier than sunrise. In some Sufi traditions, if the practitioner naturally awakens around 3 A.M., it is said that the angels are calling her or him to prayer, and it is considered a precious invitation. In the Christian monastery, the day of prayer begins with the chanting of Matins, the first hour of the Divine Office, generally around 1 A.M.; the Angelus bell rings at noon, inviting remembrance; a pause is made before beginning a meal to offer thanks.

Others will find regular and ideal times for prayer when the body has been exercised or when they have done some physical labor, so that the muscles are not crying out for attention. Circumstantially, we may find prayer the natural outpouring when we have just made love, or when we are feeling the vulnerability of our humanity for some other reason. The parent of an infant may treasure the time in which she holds a sleeping child, contemplating trust and unconditional love, as the best time to pray. But, since we can't stay in the lovemaking chamber all day, and because our infants grow into toddlers, we are wise to establish specific times for prayer that do not depend upon circumstances.

The length of our prayer time will depend upon too many factors to list. Within a structured group practice, we honor the time frame set up beforehand. When left to our own devices, I strongly advocate that we give ourselves a schedule of prayer, rather than simply going with the flow. This flow method can easily deteriorate into the sense that we can only pray when we feel that something good is going on—an entirely subjective and unreliable gauge of the value of our prayer. Establish a minimal time period—like twenty minutes or one hour, depending upon your desire and your need—and stick to it, no matter what. You can always increase the time as you wish, but don't shorten it, especially if you find yourself trying the excuse that you are bored, tired or a failure at this program.

Some people are tempted to terminate prayer because it is simply too intense or too scary, or because they are experiencing physical overtones, like trembling or shortness of breath. Such indicators are rarely dangerous if we don't try to increase them as some means of getting high, which is not the point of prayer. Nevertheless, if you have a guide or a teacher, which I highly recommend, it is essential to speak to them about such phenomena. In the moment, however, simply observe whatever is going on without drawing conclusions, as much as you can. Call upon God's help to guide you in what to do or not do next. Change your focus, perhaps by chanting the name of God. Focus on your breath, and keep your focus there instead of in your thoughts and projections about what this phenomenon might mean. And, particularly if you don't have a teacher or a guide to back you up, it may be best to simply get up and move around, putting your attention on something else for a while.

The point is that we are learning and looking for times and ways and means in which our access to the other domain is strongest and most viable. We are attempting to move into this other domain and to hang out there, to feed from the tables laid out, to rest, to absorb the light. And we will only learn this by doing it.

As to establishing a place of prayer, a place in our home, once again I'm all for it. After all, we set up entertainment centers in our family room, don't we? We set up breakfast nooks and studios and offices and workout rooms, each with their paraphernalia and consequent ambiance. Shouldn't we at least have a meditation corner in our bedroom or in a closet, or dedicate a small room in our homes as our chapel or meditation space—a place in which we can set up an altar, or stare at a blank wall without distraction, or look out a window into the garden, or keep a cushion on the floor, or position our meditation chair? Creating a place that invites the mood of prayer is the whole point. That place then becomes a powerful reminding factor for us, drawing us back to the renewal of intention. It also stores our prayer-energy, empowering whatever artifacts we may have there. Used consistently, our meditation seat literally becomes a source of help to us. An image of the Divine—a picture, a sculpture, an object from nature—becomes a sanctuary and a vessel for the Deity itself.

Whatever is generated in our place of prayer can spread to other objects and other places, helping us to maintain our prayer life on the road as we travel, at the office, in our parent's condo when we visit them for the weekend, or in the classroom as we teach the next algebra lesson. I have a thin red fabric from India that I drape around my neck as a scarf when I take a long-distance flight. Nobody needs to know that this scarf is sometimes a covering for my altar at home, but I can't forget that it is soaked with years of prayer. Buying a few fresh flowers and putting them anywhere is always a reminder of the place of prayer, and a silent form of invocation. How simply could you turn your car or your office into a place of prayer and meditation? You get the point.

On the other hand, we want to be warriors in the life of prayer. We must be able to pray wherever we are, under any circumstances. Like Etty Hillesum, the young Dutch woman who spent several years in Nazi detention camps prior to being sent to Auschwitz, we can learn to see the beauty of the night sky even when it shines above a barbed wire fence. We can learn to interiorize our place of prayer so clearly that we can take it with us, anywhere, and live from within that place, no matter how difficult the external circumstances.

And finally, as to method, well, here again it all depends …
Prayer methods are numerous—a function of circumstance, of
personal liking, of spiritual tradition, of age and experience, of
a teacher's direction. As children, we prayed as children, asking for things. As adults we can pray as lovers, as responsible
and trustworthy knights and ladies of the monarch, as instruments in the hand of the great artist. Every book and every
teacher of prayer has a method to offer, and you will certainly
find a few suggested in this small volume. I will share with
you the non-method method that I have learned over time
from my own teacher. I will write about invoking the name
of God as a means of constantly focusing one's life energy on
what matters. I will tell stories of people who prayed dangerously, and include their prayers for your inspiration, and I will
invite you to write your prayers as an adjunct to other methods
of prayer. And, through it all, I will urge you to settle on a
method or non-method and to stick with it until the method
itself dissolves, or until it becomes obvious (outside of your
disinclination based in boredom) that it is time to move into
another approach.

Many many years can be wasted in flitting from one type
of prayer or practice to another. Flitting around is probably a
necessary stage, for a while. Perhaps it will convince us that
superficial involvements, like one-night stands, don't afford
the long-term satisfaction we crave. Those who have walked
the mystical path ahead of us warn of the danger of making
a lot of side trips. Spiritual materialism abounds today, and
is seen vividly at work in the smorgasbord of approaches to
prayer and practice. If you go Sufi dancing tonight and sit
zazen in the morning, and pray your rosary in the afternoon,
and chant with the Hari Krishnas on Saturdays and go to the
Native American pow-wows on Sundays, you *may* in fact be

a highly-evolved soul, a pure and universal spirit. But, chances are much more likely that you are a mere dabbler, and a seeker after highs, and that you collect prayer methods and prayer experiences the way your neighbor collects antique cars or the kid down the block collects beer bottles from around the world. The spiritual dilettante tastes it all, but commits to none of it.

Method is a straightjacket. It is meant to tie us down. It is meant to force us to find the tiny trapdoor that lies at the bottom of the soul. Methods aren't necessarily supposed to be fun, even though sometimes they are; or bliss-filled, even though sometimes they are. Methods help us to see more clearly the vague bars of illusion that we generally live behind. Methods help us to cut through our denial systems, by pushing our noses against them. Method gives direction and sanity in the midst of chaos. Method provides a framework in which one person's intention is aligned with the intentions of others, thereby strengthening the intention and the prayer it invokes. Method is a magic carpet, carrying us to the heart of God. Those who, by their own admission, are finally liberated from the confines of method, witness to the value of method over and over again. They continue in their methods because they have learned that "form is emptiness and emptiness is form." They warn us that we can't be free of method until we have mastered method.

In my own practice I too dabbled around for years. I chose breadth of understanding rather than depth of involvement. I tried to get the teaching about prayer by having my questions answered about it. You don't learn to pray by first learning about prayer, and you don't learn self-observation by imagining the difficulties that will arise when you do practice it, and then asking for ways to circumvent these difficulties. You learn prayer and self-observation by praying and self-observing, with diligence and commitment, and then asking questions based in your experience about what you are practicing.

For years I heard that chanting the name of God was a powerful means of transformation. Until I dedicated myself to doing this method, however, all my questions and considerations about it were mere speculation. Method here meant establishing a time and place for implementing what was merely a good idea but not a reality. The method was hard work. Over time, the practice developed a life of its own. The method still endures, but the rigidity surrounding it has transformed.

The idea that we can ignite an inner life by an occasional reference to "all is God," is a naïve notion. You don't ignite the inner life by plugging in your Zen water garden and gazing at the moon, although that can certainly feed an already blazing intention. An inner life of prayer, like any life of mastery, requires that prayer becomes one's obsession—God becomes the obsession, truth becomes the obsession. The inner life is ignited and kept aflame when everything that doesn't nurture that obsession is discarded—from the twenty minutes here spent browsing fashion magazines, to the half-an-hour there spent advising a friend who never follows our advice anyway, to the hours spent in worry and fear about anything. When our day becomes a form of serving our obsession with God, we have entered into the real stream of prayer, and we are fanning the inner life. Then, all our decisions are answered in the light of what serves our work and what doesn't. Our only concern is the degree to which one activity will encourage our aim over against another activity. When in doubt, we take our best guess. And, when we choose brief respite from our obsession, when we choose indulgence in self-pity or self-comfort, we gently and calmly tell ourselves the truth about that, and move ahead without judgement. In that way, our entire life—from waking up until waking up, and every second in between, even our failure to live this way—is guided by its orientation toward the north star of God, and by whatever will build the inner life.

V

# Working with the Mind

We come to prayer desiring a certain communion, even if we don't know what form that communion will take. But, what do we typically find when we begin to pray? We find the patterns of a lifetime—a lifetime of mental habits. Mind—our dearest friend and most bitter enemy; the source of brilliant insight and great ideas, as well as the source of our suffering. We soon realize that there is a monster ravaging this interior temple that we had hoped to keep clean and quiet. We may call this monster by any name—obsession, worry, internal debate, doubt, fantasy, discontent ... whatever—almost all of it, however, is painful and distressing, at least in the sense that it draws us away from life as it is. When the monster is raging we focus all our attention upon it. We tighten up around some issue or a question that the mind is stuck on. The body contracts. That issue or question seems like the only thing on the horizon. Our vision narrows. The issue takes on great importance; its resolution becomes a struggle between life or death. "Hey, wait a minute," we protest when we realize what is happening, "I came here to pray not to drown in this swamp."

I was on retreat with the pure intention of praying for others. Yet, the very intention to pray became a source of consternation. How best to pray? What forms? What words? And should I chant for an hour or say my mantra, or just sit? Within a few seconds of beginning my formal prayer, I was caught again in a labyrinth from which there seemed no escape. Confusion reigned. The mind was flailing about, looking for some relief, some resolution.

Thoughts have power. The longer we hold them without recognizing that we are identifying with their implications, the more firmly they become entrenched. Worry unchecked feeds more worry. The body suffers the results. The soul is denied its nourishment. It is all a vicious circle.

Many meditation practices offer a centering device—like a mantra, or a centering prayer, or an internal visualization, or a watching of the breath—as a means of corralling the wild mind. The practice that I have been given by my teacher involves simply witnessing what is arising in the mind without trying to change it. The key in this approach is the mood of softness in which the arising is held. One observes without judgement, and when judgement does occur, one observes that judgement without judgement. The body remains in an erect sitting posture throughout. No matter how torrential the rain of thoughts, no matter how forceful, we hold our seat and watch what arises, doing nothing.

By observing and yet not moving, we take a step back from complete identification with what is occurring. Over time, the spaciousness we give to the arising thoughts increases. The vision is no longer so narrow. The thoughts continue, but the field in which they play is more vast. They are smaller, less insistent, by virtue of being put in context. Sort of like what happens when you give a wild horse a larger corral. "Take a friendly attitude toward your thoughts," Chögyam Trungpa Rinpoche, the great Tibetan master would say, capturing the essence of what is needed to live with the mind, yet not be run by it.

These very thoughts—our obsessions in all their forms—can also be invitations to prayer. Confusion and distress can become loud alarm clocks that alert us to the presence of old habits, habits of giving power to thoughts; habits of robbing our life energy by identification. When the alarm clock rings, what better moment for prayer?

Back to my experience on retreat, I realized that my dilemma about how to pray was no different from my dilemma about money, or my health, or my friend's opinion of me, or my husband's dirty socks on the bedroom floor, or whatever else occupies my mind. In that recognition, I took the contents of mind and wrapped them all together into a lovely package. I tied a bow around my gift and I brought it to the feet of the Lord. "Here," I said, "you take it. This is all I have to offer You in this moment. Here is my prayer, as poor as it is. It is all Yours, anyway. My inability to pray, my inability to remember You, is Yours."[1]

Then, I watched what arose; and whatever happened, I gave it more space.

The bottom line is that our perceptions, no matter how much they may generate internal turmoil, are insubstantial, like dust in the wind. Thoughts and feelings are energetic phenomena, but *we are not* our thoughts and feelings. They come, they go. They rise, they subside. They change, and change and change. Ultimately, our perceptions cannot separate us from the One we rest in. We *do* rest in God, and God *does* live in us. We are not separate, and never can be separate. But, we forget this. We can get stuck for years, even lifetimes, in believing our perceptions, in identifying with our thoughts and feelings, and based in this belief and identification, we can create a fortress of defense, upholding our imagined separation even with our dying breath.

Let's not wait that long to drop our guns.

# THE BODY IN PRAYER

My friend is in deep pain. Her husband has left her. The husband's son, whom she has mothered since he was three, is a teenager now, on his way to college. My friend is alone, suddenly. She aches in her aloneness.

I want to serve her, but my words, as true as they are objectively, drop like rocks from my mouth. They are hard. They are frozen. She reaches for them, but they are too heavy to lift and too cold to touch. I'd like to be able to serve her in a way that matters. I sit on the edge of her bed and take her in my arms, silently. I hold her.

Briefly, as I hold my friend, the thought and the spontaneous prayer arises, "O God, be comfort and strength to her. O God, let Your love heal her, give her courage, give her joy. Please help me to practice in my life that I may liberate my own mind from its prison of illusion so that I may serve others in this liberation." But, for most of the time I am simply quiet within. Nothing is happening, except that my body is praying the prayer of holding a friend in need.

When my friend first suffered the shock of her separation, my teacher recommended to her that she get lots of physical contact from her women friends. His recommendation was an invitation into the body of prayer. He knows that the body is the vessel of the spirit. In and through the body we can actually locate the place in which heart resonates with Heart.

Body-prayer can be expressed as celebration, in song or dance or poetry or art; it can be expressed as nurturing or healing; it can be an act of service, it can be in the breathing in and out, in gratitude. God lives in the body, inseparable from the breath, the blood, the muscles and bone. Sometimes, when we sit or kneel to pray, or in the midst of sex, or for some totally inexplicable reason, we will simply be aware of energy, life energy, moving throughout our system. We may actually feel this life coursing through our veins; we may become aware of our *chakras* opening, of our muscles becoming enlivened, of our heart being opened. These energies are the tangible expression of aliveness, which is godliness, and as such these energies are a living prayer. They don't need something superimposed on them to make them holy, because they already are. Yet, the mind will almost always try to make some sense of them, try to adjust them, or fit them into some pattern, or glorify them, or channel them or sublimate them. Meanwhile, the aching chest may be throbbing with longing for consummation in mystery, the reality of the body in prayer. These divine energies are simply working their alchemical process in the cells.

At such times, it is well to do nothing, or as little as possible, except perhaps to renew intention: "Let *this* (without specifying what "this" is, which would only limit it) be used for the highest purposes of *sadhana* (spiritual work)" as my teacher would say; or even more simply, "Thy Will be done."

The Divine is always infusing our body with its radiance, we just don't always feel it or fall into the recognition of it. Tessa Bielecki, a Christian hermit and writer about prayer, has told us that it takes as much courage and discipline to bear the ecstasy of prayer as it does to bear the agony.[1] And both sensations do and will arise in our prayer because we have a body.

Prayer is both a means and an end. It is both the path and the goal. In the process of communication with the heart of hearts, we will build up our courage and strength to be able to bear the agony and ecstasy of life, which is God.

## THE POSTURE OF PRAYER

Years ago, when leading a workshop about health, I asked the thirty participants to join me for yoga practice from 6 to7 A.M., prior to the general morning program. Only ten women responded to the invitation. We met in the plush-carpeted living room of the seminar house, looking out at the Pacific Ocean.

After one morning of shared silence and gentle movement we were already bonding as a group, and one woman suggested that we create an altar to honor the elements—a sacred corner that would draw our attention and encourage remembrance. The next day we made our shrine, filling a table with crystals, a bowl of water, a candle, a tiny piece of driftwood—each one representative of our appreciation for the natural world.

But now that the altar was established, what were we actually going to do with it, I wondered. The women spontaneously answered my unvoiced question by gathering around it before our practice began, and by bowing in front of it as they left. Some went so far as to perform a formal *pranam*—down on knees, hands joined at the level of the chest, and then bending at the waist until the forehead was touching the floor. The gesture was not foreign to me, as I had been *pranaming* at the feet of my guru for years. These women wanted to bow, and many of them risked their initial discomfort in trying it.

Having bowed once, they apparently found it useful, as they continued the practice for each day thereafter. The gesture became a bodily prayer.

Unless one has actually made such a bow it can be a scary proposition. Yet, once accomplished, the feeling in the body is quite profound. The whole body prays when it bows. Placing oneself in the posture of surrender, that very posture becomes a means of instruction. The body teaches the mind what it feels and looks like to let go.

If the mind or ego alone were allowed to rule, one would never bow down, to anything. Many people find it absolutely abhorrent, if not heretical, to imagine such a gesture, as if in the bowing they are somehow diminished. Actually, in my experience the opposite is the case. Something is increased, but what that something is ... well, one has to do it to find out. For myself, I'd say that something rigid is relaxed in the bowing, and something is made right, as if the very posture testifies to my organic alignment as a human being within the hierarchy of creation—which is really not a hierarchy at all, but a vast web of interdependent energies. Is there a more perfect way to symbolize and thereby acknowledge one's gratitude and appreciation to the other elements in one's web of life for the constancy of their being, and for the countless blessings that their constancy affords? How generous the crystals and feathers have been and are! How wondrous the pounding ocean waves, endless night skies, the mountains! And how deserving of honor, and even worship such things are. How incomprehensible have been the sacrifices and the offerings of countless humans who have lived before us, to say nothing of those who live now, whose precious life energy has been spent in sewing our clothes, cultivating our rice, sifting the sand for our cement.

We need to bow to one another. We can well afford to prostrate ourselves at the feet of our brothers and sisters and lovers, and before our sacred symbols representative of the infinite, unnamable One, and certainly before our gurus or teachers. We need to bow down, to prostrate, fully, to the Divine alive in and with and through ourselves too.

I once spent a weekend in prayer in which we were directed to pray in all different postures. For the first fifteen minutes of each hour we stood. For the second fifteen minutes we knelt. For the third we did the traditional Indian *pranam*, forehead to the ground, and for the fourth quarter we prostrated fully, stretched out full length, with hands as a pillow to the forehead. After a while the body found its rhythm, and the movement from fully erect to completely prone became a dance. Each posture engendered a slightly different energy current in the body. Each posture was a slightly different prayer.

It is important to know that, no matter what posture we are in, prayer is possible. It is important to pray in every posture and under every situation. It is essential to always be bowing to everything, even if that bow is not expressed. To bow to the feet of the clerk in the store would probably not serve. But, to bow to the other in the heart seems to be a way to live in constant gratitude and respect.

The great Zen master, Suzuki Roshi, has a similar take on the subject of bowing, recorded in his book *Zen Mind, Beginner's Mind.* He says that "by bowing we are giving up ourselves." And that, "To give up ourselves is to give up our dualistic ideas"—the notions that we are somehow separate from anything.[2] We are the Buddha, the Roshi instructs. Buddha simply bows to Buddha. He says: "When you bow to Buddha you should have no idea of Buddha, you just become one with Buddha, you are already Buddha himself."[3]

The poet Kabir strikes a resonant chord when he says:

The spiritual master arrives and bows down to the beginning student, try to live to see this![4]

There is no separation—between master and student, between myself and God. To "live to see this" is to know that. What a help it is to see this reality enacted in form. In the church, the priest enters and bows to the congregation before beginning the service, and several times throughout the ritual. In the meditation hall, the master enters and the students bow, and then the master bows to the students. The same happens on the mat when one is practicing martial arts. The teacher bows to the student, the students bow to the teacher. All things are in rightful relationship to one another.

Every day I bow to my teacher as a sign of respect. On Sunday nights for over twenty-five years, in the formal service of *darshan*, I presented him with a handful of fruits or an array of fresh flowers, symbols of the fruits of the earth and the fruits of my interior garden, of which he is the gardener. I was simply returning to him what he had given me, returning to God what God has given me. And, after the presentation, I placed my head to the floor at his feet, or touched the ground upon which he walked, thus enacting the giving up of myself and my notions of separation. I thus bowed to the One; I bowed to my teacher who was not separate from that One; I bowed to myself, in recognition that I am not separate from that One.

When I raised my head from this posture of bowing, my teacher's hand was always extended toward me. His hand contained a gift to me, his continual feeding, his nurturance, his blessing, and his expression of surrender to me. Usually he offered a sweet—a piece of candy or a cookie. "Taste and see how good is the Lord," I might reflect. This line from the Psalms is made real when I savor the *prasad*, the sacred offering that is returned to me.

My teacher once shared that we are closest to the essence of our being when we are *pranaming*. When we are bowing we are closest to who we really are.

Good posture or correct posture allows the breath to move in a way that is balanced, it thus allows the breath itself to naturally flow as prayer. An erect posture that is both dignified and relaxed creates a link in the human between the heavens and the earth. Posture of this type is a reflection of an inner state of Divine elegance and an expression of Divine pride, in which one is willing to own one's place in this amazing lineage of one's religious tradition, and in the lineage of life.

The aligned posture of prayer makes one available to channel higher energies onto or into the earth, as the mystic Gurdjieff taught about prayer, and as many of us realize from our experience of yoga and prayer. Consciously assumed, posture is a reflection of attention and awareness to the present moment—a sign that one is alive on the spot. Many people have the discipline to go to a health club to work out, but when they come home they sit and move in a manner that says, "I don't respect myself." The observation and the maintenance of good posture provides a built-in means of self-discipline and thus self-respect. One chooses to assume control over the body, rather than being at the effect of the mind's demand for a stressless (read "dead") existence.

Knowing how one's body is located in space in any moment is a sign that we are awake in that moment. If we are in the house and we know that we are in the house, we are halfway there to being present to whatever takes place in the

house. It is amazing how many moments of our lives we literally don't know that we are in the house. Every time we sit up
in our chair, or every moment that we straighten our back and
ground ourselves on our meditation cushion or step onto our
yoga mat, we are making a choice for presence, for consciousness, for owning our birthright as humans on earth. Are we
too busy to observe and work with posture? Then we are too
busy in general. The body in alignment, conscious of its position in space, is a body in prayer.

I recently began a serious practice of hatha yoga, after having dabbled in this discipline for decades. Now, at least twice
a week, I join others at a local yoga studio and relearn how to
use my body as a living prayer. As I breathe and stretch and
establish a firm foundation in my legs and feet, I praise God, I
praise life and thereby reenter the sanctuary of my own body,
my vehicle for serving God's will.

The type of yoga I study is called Anusara Yoga, and its
methodologies are never purely physical. Always we use the
postures as means of building this internal temple; as a means
of recognizing and reanimating our highest aim in all aspects
of life. And so, before we begin our practice we join our hands,
palm facing palm, at the level of the heart, and we chant *Om
nama shivaya gurave* ... an invocation that awakens us to the
reality that we *are* that light, which is the source of all. For me,
having spent all my adult life attempting to integrate spirituality into everyday life, the addition of this precious discipline
is a gift that I hope to never stop honoring.

The attempt of the yoga practice is to attune the body-
mind to the universal flow of energy. When one "feels into" or
listens intently, both *within* and *without*, one "hears" (i.e, experiences) the song of praise and gratitude that is inherent in
creation. The human heart and mind is naturally overwhelmed,

awestruck, when it sees and hears and tastes and smells things as they truly are. Unexpectedly, one breath of sweet spring air, one dazzling view of a desert sky on fire with the sunset, one unearned smile from a child, and even the most hardened atheist connects to a modicum of gratitude for something ... call it "beauty," or merely "serendipity." The only prerequisite to such gratitude is the possibility of seeing what is, in any given moment. It is this condition of awe/gratitude that spontaneously erupts into praise.

## THE RELAXATION THAT IS PRAYER

Years ago, I took a short trip with my teacher. When I asked him what time we should leave for the airport he suggested a time that was later than I had expected. With a rush of panic I vexed over how to tactfully suggest that we leave earlier. Instead of being straight about it, I left him a note asking if he would like me to take the car out the night before to get it filled with gas, so that we wouldn't have to stop on the way to the airport.

My obvious manipulation and the fear it attempted to cover were not lost to him. I got my note back a few hours later. In large letters he had written on it, "RELAX, My Father is taking care of everything," a reference to his own complete reliance on the direction of his life by the grace of his guru, Yogi Ramsuratkumar. He was inviting me into the same.

Could I do it? Well, let's put it this way, I could relinquish the external activities associated with my worry, I could give up on the idea of getting gas ahead of time and abide the departure time he had set up. But relax, really relax—that was a different story. I couldn't make myself relax, but I could make gestures of relaxation and orient myself in that direction. I could sit still rather than running around trying to be helpful, which often results in stepping on toes. Even though I might be fuming and fretting inside, I could hold myself in place. I could breathe slowly and deeply to calm myself down. I could watch the scenarios created in my mind—like the scenario at the airport with myself quarreling with the ticket agent to get us on the next plane—and refuse to identify with these scenarios as being ultimately the last word on the situation, or on myself. Sitting still, doing nothing about anything, a certain resignation began to dawn: "Ah, what the hell. What's the worst that could happen? We'll miss the plane and get to see what comes next."

We didn't miss the plane, of course. In fact we were extraordinarily early.

I framed that little slip of paper on which that reminder to RELAX had been written. I attached it to my computer monitor. It became a part of my life. The invitation to relax, I've learned, had much more to do with developing a deep trust, a radical reliance, in the ongoing Providence of God than it did with perfecting any stress management techniques. This sitting still, along with observation of the mind, however, was for me a necessary prelude to the deeper resting in and trusting the Divine that was to come later.

Resting and trusting is what begins to effect a transformation of one's life, but it's like one can't get there from here—I can't rest and trust until I know that I am not resting and trusting. Otherwise, I just keep overlaying more good ideas about rest and trust on an uptight and overwrought nervous system. And, I've acutely experienced the sad results of that overlaying in my body—with headaches and skin rashes, to name a few. The body knows what's genuine relaxation and what isn't.

Is it any wonder that prayer, with its promise of deep resting in the heart of the Divine, is both enormously compelling and extraordinarily difficult? Prayer is difficult because we often need a lot of time to unwind. We may come to prayer hoping for immediate relief and instead, even when the body is stilled, we may find a wild mind that whips us around inside as effectively as any hurricane whips the trees. It takes time to see our strategies of over-control and manipulation of everything, and how those strategies are illusory attempts to dam up the river of Divine Providence that is always washing over us, flooding our territory—our heart.

The being longs for the possibility of itself in deep rest, simply drowning in the Beloved's waves. Yet the strategies we enact to discourage what we say we want most are enormous. And, what is even more daunting is that the work to be done *is* so unending and so challenging. It seems to call for a type of vigilance and heroic effort that undermines our ability to relax.

So, here we are again, apparently back at square one in our attempt to solve the enigma of prayer in the midst of an active life of service. We are constantly being gifted with the overwhelming tasks of incarnation and with the furtherance of God's work on earth, while at the same time being called into a new context, a context in which all that work is done from relaxation, from the heart. It's a tough one.

This *koan* doesn't get solved in the mind, however. It only gets solved in the midst of life. One actually learns to find the heart of silence and the place of deep rest even as war is raging. That's part of the warrior's job—to never lose his head no matter how dreadful the circumstances and to make all his efforts seem effortless. But, even that sounds like hard hard work, which it is, and may lead us to forget that there is another factor in the equation, namely, that God is in charge of the whole play. The more reliable and consistent our practice becomes, the more we gain clarity that our lives are being moved by God, not by our own manipulations.

We create a tremendous amount of suffering for ourselves because we are not willing to get off our position of needing to control everything. But, until we can see we are doing this, we will just keep doing it in more and more sophisticated ways. Prayer gives us the chance to pause long enough to blow the whistle on our own strategies.

Prayer is a lot like waiting for a bus that is already late. If we leave the bus stop to do something else while we wait, we run the risk of missing it when it finally comes. If we stand around complaining to the other people at the bus stop, we do nothing but spend a lot of precious life energy, and increase our impatience and boredom besides. If we read a good book, or write a letter or sit still, stay in place and watch the mind, we maximize our time. By the time the bus gets there we can actually enjoy the ride, we can relax into our seat. We are ready for what comes next.

So, what can be said about relaxation and prayer? First, that prayer happens or arises naturally, bubbling up to the surface, as the body relaxes its stranglehold on survival and control. Second, that this relaxation has nothing to do with wearing soft casual clothing, laying in a hot tub or sipping a chilled glass of white wine at the end of a hard day. Certainly all these activities do relax the body in small ways, and they can create a point of reference for how the body feels when it has dropped some of its control, for how enjoyable it is when the internal critical-parent isn't running the whole show. However, one can't create a walking hot-tub without developing wrinkled and water-logged skin. One can't keep drinking wine all day and all night without consequences that may create exactly the opposite effect. One can't have a twenty-four-hour-a-day massage, even though some would like to try. So, the form and the source of our relaxation must be of an entirely different order. When we relax the grasping mind, the body relaxes. Therefore, we work on relaxation from the inside out—we sit in a designated posture, a straight posture, a posture that discourages sleep and indulgence, and we learn to relax inside the straightness.

Third, the kind of relaxation we crave is the relaxation of a child in its mother's arms, or as D.H. Lawrence has so beautifully expressed it, "like a cat asleep on a chair at peace, ... at one with the master of the house."[5] A perfect analogy to prayer. The relaxation of the child or that of the cat is one of deep bodily satisfaction and security. This child is taken care of, protected. This cat is safe, at peace. What a lovely starting point in our prayer—to know that we live in the presence of the Divine Mother, or rest in the hands of the Master of Creation. What a difference such knowing would create in the way we live our lives.

One who knows this place of rest and relaxation can venture boldly into areas of risk-taking. One doesn't need to stay curled up on the couch. One gets on about one's day. As Tessa Bielecki has told us, we can't have constant "bedroom mysticism." Neither can we be constantly suckling at the Divine Mother's breast. She wants us to suckle what we need until we are strong enough to be about our business (our "Father's business," as Jesus said). The trouble is, we may leave the Mother's breast to stand on our own but we may forget the bond that this suckling has actually established—the bond of love. Instead, we may assume a new posture, one that leads to rigidity. The posture we more commonly take is one based in the assumption of non-love.

In prayer we have the opportunity to re-experience and strengthen that bond of love, that degree of restful security, knowing ourselves to be beloved of God the Mother. Or, we may deepen that bond by simply experiencing our interrelatedness with all things.

We can only begin.

## THE PATH IS THE GOAL

So often where the spiritual life is concerned we develop a warrior's stance. We make our prayer into a type of crusade. We discipline ourselves to prayer. We pray through the dryness, no matter what. This is all well and good provided it does not overshadow the other side. It can be downright pleasurable to pray, to rest in God, to leisurely explore the domains of love, like enjoying a long afternoon of foreplay.

I am reminded of the phrase "the path is the goal," which was explained so well in a book by the same name, written by the Tibetan Master, Chögyam Trungpa Rinpoche.[1] Applied to our consideration of praying dangerously we can say that the very act of prayer is an expression of one's alignment with the life of prayer that may be the desired goal. The point is that when we are praying we are *being* that which we seek. Time ceases to limit us. We simply manifest ourselves in and as the condition that we aim for.

How blessed to remove a prize from the end of the rainbow. How joyous to have nothing to reward us *then*. How wondrous to be *now* a living, breathing prayer. "This is it," as the old Zen Master says, "nothing comes next."

Perhaps we could consider that we don't need to "do" prayer the way we "do" the dishes. That prayer is not something that we finish so we can start fresh again. Rather, we pray because prayer is its own reward. Or because prayer is our rightful, aligned state. We don't breathe to finish something, do we?

In some schools of Buddhist practice a great deal of emphasis is placed on sitting meditation. The sitting has no end in and of itself, although it has consequences. The sitting is simply an expression of alignment with life; a state of non-resistance to what is. I have heard it said that the Buddha sits on the meditation pillow, meaning that when the practitioner is in her rightful place she *is* the Buddha. That's all. To practice is not to become enlightened. To practice is to express the inherent enlightenment that is always ours.

Our prayer is the expression of our divinity, or our "intrinsic dignity and intrinsic nobility" as the Indian master Swami Prajnanpad has said. When we are in our rightful posture and place of prayer, whether that is remembering God as we get into the car, or whether we are falling to our knees in awe before the high altar in the great cathedral, with the pipe organ resounding a Mozart prelude—we *are* the Lord, or the Goddess, or the Beloved to whom we pray. Our prayer is the expression of our faith, our love, our yearning, and even our humanity with all its fears and insecurities.

Recently, as I approached the gate to my teacher's ashram, stopped the car and slowly moved my long cramped legs out onto the dirt drive, the sheer joy of rising to stand sent a shiver of joy through my body. I realized that I was living the life that I longed to live in that moment—I wasn't living to get anywhere else. This moment, this body, this breath was all there was; it was enough.

VII

# INVISIBLE PRAYER

The Little Brothers (and Sisters) of Charles de Foucauld are a Christian community of nobodys. Some of them live in the poorest sections of a city, others in poor villages, invisibly moving among their neighbors. By day, they work in the same factories or fields as their neighbors do. By night, they retreat to solitary rooms or huts to spend hours in silent and contemplative prayer, loving the God who has called them to this austere vocation, lost to the eyes of the world. Failures all.

This life of complete anonymity and invisible service to those who meet them and to those they will never see, thrilled me from the first time I heard of this community of men and women. In contrast to the approach of many religious and spiritual disciplines, which urge a sort of radical witness to holiness, to service, to sharing the name of God—all of which can be wondrous celebrations and necessary functions—these nobodys and hundreds like them, faceless saints, are lost to God alone, and probably create a much-needed energetic balance in the great body of creation.

By way of background, Charles de Foucauld was a Trappist monk, not a priest but a simple monk. He had chosen the poorest Trappist monastery in existence, that of Akbes in Syria, in which to carry out the mission of his life—to pray. One day, his abbot sent him to keep vigil by the corpse of a poor man who had recently died. When Brother

Charles entered the dead man's shack he was confronted with real poverty, and touched by it as never before. Here were genuinely hungry children and a weak and defenseless widow without assurance of the next day's bread. It was this spiritual crisis which called him to leave the monastery of Trappists and go in search of a religious life very different from the earlier one. De Foucauld wrote:

> We, who have chosen the imitation of Jesus and Jesus Crucified, are very far from the trials, the pains, the insecurity and the poverty to which these people are subjected. I no longer want a monastery which is too secure. I want a small monastery, like the house of a poor workman who is not sure if tomorrow he will find work and bread, who with all his being shares the suffering of the world. O Jesus, a monastery like your house at Nazareth, in which to live hidden as you did when you came among us.[1]

With de Foucauld as our inspiration here, I suggest that those intent on cultivating prayer as a way of life should remind themselves of the dangers of becoming accomplished "pray-ers," visible witnesses to prayer.

I gave a workshop a few years ago on the subject of gratitude. The participants were drawn from all walks of life. When I asked people to introduce themselves to the group, one man startled me by declaring that he was a contemplative, that he had studied prayer with so and so, and had been practicing this and that discipline for so many years … I felt quite embarrassed for him, as the others in the group listened politely without reaction. It is so easy to take a position of holiness, or identify with one's desire to be a contemplative or mystic, or even to encourage others to see us as the man of prayer or woman of prayer whom we aspire to be. At the same time, however, false humility is as deadly as spiritual pride. We can't and shouldn't strategize to be invisible, silent, soft-spoken, thereby hoping to leave others wondering about the glories of our inner life. Knowing that such traps are always waiting for us, on either side of the line, we are sensible to be on guard. Overall, we are probably a lot safer in remaining silent than in trying to promote a prayer life to others.

There *is* a time and a place to witness, but there is the more necessary time and place to drop no clues, leave no traces. I think the higher practice is to have an invisible spiritual life. Not that you deliberately act anti-spiritual, whatever that may mean to you—take up cigar-smoking in church, swear at unsuspecting old ladies and children, use bibles for doorstops, for instance. But, certainly, any drawing of attention to your prayerfulness is a surefire means of undermining whatever you are attempting to build. "Don't cast your pearls before swine," Jesus advised us. Employ no gestures that mark you for the spiritual type.

I can speak about such spiritual posturing because I've been an accomplished spiritualite for long years of my adult life. God help me, I have a lot to be unburdened of. In my twenties I was a nun, and I will admit that I got a lot of acknowledgement out of wearing that habit … I still do in fact, although I dropped that habit a long time ago. In my thirties I was part of an Indian sect that wore only orange and red clothing. I recall with remorse going to visit my parents at their home during that time, and being highly insulted when my Dad asked me not to perform my Tai Chi exercises on the front lawn of the house in the sight of the whole neighborhood. (*Awooh*, that memory still hurts!) Over time I have learned through hard knocks and humiliation that the idea is to really *have* an inner life, not to rub people's noses in it, or to hint at having a secret life just enough to impress people.

If my inner life is so tentative that I can't live it invisibly, internally, for three days in a hotel room that I am sharing with a friend or acquaintance without the need to set up a shrine or get up at 4 A.M. to pray for a few hours, thus drawing attention to myself and serving to discomfort my companions, then my inner life isn't "inner" at all. Maybe it's time to cultivate a life of prayer that can go anywhere, do almost anything, and still be full of fire.

Besides the fact that it is just good manners not to be boasting of one's inner life, there is another reason to keep such practices discrete. My friend Lalitha, who has been a mentor for many years, calls this discretion "accumulating substances for *sadhana.*" In the cosmology of praying dangerously we consider that prayer generates an energetic substance that is able to be stored within the body. Once accumulated, that energetic substance can be directed to where it may be needed: it may be offered on the altar of the Divine as a tangible gift; it may be contained within the body, where it effects a subtle but affirmative alchemy; it may be directed to those in need throughout the world.

This prayer substance acts as a building material to strengthen the energetic pathways in the whole body, allowing the body to channel and contain the enormous stresses that life offers to those who seek to serve with a capital "S," and increasing the body's capacity to contain more, thereby rendering it more useful as a transformer. But, just as it can be contained, such substance can also be frittered away, leaked by small and large measure. "Loose lips sink ships," the old saying goes. We do it all the time, which is the reason that our prayer life might not be gelled for us. It may be that we get a hit of the substance of God, and we feel so good, so liberated, so desirous of more such substance that instead of holding quietly with what we have, we dissipate what we have stored by our enthusiastic proclamations about it. We talk about our revelations and inspirations, and get all excited about them. We start polishing our halo. Such celebration becomes the ego's excuse to lessen the vigilance of our practice. After all, we think, since we're progressing so admirably we might as well reward ourselves a bit. And in that celebration we effectively take the substance of prayer and waste it. We don't *mean* to lose it, quite the opposite. We want to save it and build on it. But, we are like compulsive shoppers. We are just undisciplined and shortsighted. We prefer the quick fix to the long-term transformation.

We also blow off our accumulated prayer energy because we are afraid of the power it contains. Sometimes we are scared of these feelings, or we suspect that such internal heat will lead to our annihilation if we let it grow. We are simply afraid of what such energy will ignite if we let it smolder. We dread the idea of anything disrupting our habitual lifestyle, even if we say we want God alone.

It is understandable. It takes courage to pray dangerously. Pray for that courage, and when you get it, as you will, then keep it to yourself.

# VIII

# DANGEROUS PRAYERS

"I wanted a prayer," Barbara told me. "I had not been raised to pray, and when I experienced God for the first time as an adult I had no words for that. I actually had a problem with the idea of saying words to God."

As we hiked the dry rocky trail in northern Arizona at 5:30 one morning, the first light was breaking over the mountains. The rarified air drew our conversation out clearly. There was no hesitancy in speaking about prayer to one another.

Barbara went on, "After years, I met a woman who embodied prayer for me. When I was very low she would simply and naturally invite me to pray, or she would suggest that I place my pain at the feet of God as my offering. Nothing more. This was very helpful to me, and after that I wanted to have a prayer, something I could actually *say*, every day. I wanted it very much.

"One day my husband had a conversation with our spiritual teacher and he shared my desire. The next day I received a special prayer from my teacher, and now I say this prayer each day. It is very important to me."

"Do you still have trouble with using words for prayer," I asked her.

"I don't worry about it anymore. Sometimes I pray with words, sometimes with silence, but my heart is aimed in the same direction either way. That first prayer was an invitation to begin my further exploration into prayer. I don't know where it will go, but I'm glad to be on it."

Some people I've talked to are reticent to pray in any formal way, or to use words to pray, for a variety of reasons. Many, like Barbara, never learned the words as children and are not inclined to start such a practice now. Others learned too many words. For them, the saying of prayers is associated with a childish relationship with a father- or mother-God to whom they must beg for some favor—something they are ready to abandon. There may be fear associated with saying formal prayers, since many of us were given a fear-based orientation to some "God in the sky" who might punish us if we didn't pray. I suspect that still more of us refrain from saying prayers because we can't quite believe that the Absolute Almighty God Principle could possibly be touched, let alone communicated with, by our paltry words.

So, there are many "good" reasons and innumerable excuses for not praying, with or without words. Yet, let's be honest, they all come from a mind-set, or a set of beliefs, about prayer, and, as I've learned so many times over the years, the mind is a very poor guide in the spiritual life ... at least the mind that believes its own projections; or a mind uninstructed by the genuine prayer teachings of the foundational religious traditions; or a mind that is unintegrated with the body.

We can pray dangerously with words or without words. And, words can really help at times. Words can be sacraments—holy signs of a deeper reality. They can be doorways through which we enter into mystery, into ritual, into exaltation and praise, and ultimately into the domain of wordlessness.

The words that follow are all potentially dangerous prayers. Many of them will be so familiar to you that you may at first be tempted to gloss over them—like the opening line of the Prayer of St. Francis, "Lord, make me an instrument of Thy Peace" or "Thy Will be Done," which we find as a basis of prayer in every world religion. Don't be fooled, however. Some of these prayers are familiar because they express universal truths. They represent the genuine cries of humanity in its invocation of God. They are dangerous words when they are finally received by the whole body, not just acknowledged by the mind and filed away for future reference. Remember what it is like to *feel* the full impact of a line of prayer, or a familiar maxim of the spiritual life— like "God loves you," or "God is within," for example? When my friend Antonia was dying of bone cancer, I visited her frequently during the last months of her life. I'll never forget the day that I walked into her room to find her face glowing with radiance, and a tangible sense of Divine Presence filling her tiny bedroom.

"Regina," she said, with a joyful urgency that captured my full attention. She reached out to take my hand as if she wanted to take me somewhere, to see something very important. "Regina, God ... *is* ... love. God *is* love!" she repeated with such enthusiasm and innocence that my eyes filled with tears. In that instant, she *knew* what those words meant. They were no longer concepts, but living breathing realities.

Such words, when they are finally opened to us, are completely new. When open, they *have* never been heard before. When the soul is deeply rested enough, focused, trusting, vulnerable, urgently in need, or simply graced for no good reason, she can be swallowed up in those words. She can hardly even speak them, because they become too precious, too intimate to say in polite company. Even if the words are not yet fully open to us, however, we could do a lot worse than to simply pray these words in faith.

For me, such prayers are like picking up the phone count-less times during the day and even through the night, estab-lishing a connection with the Divine. They keep the Divine Reality in the forefront of my awareness. They replace the ordinarily dreamy unconscious state in which I walk around with a state of alertness, receptivity, open-eyed clarity; namely, with conscious appreciation that all is in God and God is in all. To pray these words carefully, letting the meaning of them sink deeply into the soil of my soul, is to establish my life as an act of contemplation. There is no end to the meaning that can be drawn up from the well of these words.

Praying these prayers is about relying completely on the Divine, throwing my precious, personal life away, and letting myself become a vehicle whereby God's Presence is enlivened in the world. The one who prays such words wantonly, with-out ceasing, becomes a lightning rod of Divine Presence, in every waking moment bringing this miracle called "God" to earth and keeping it here for everyone's benefit and a means whereby the human being praises the source of all.

The prayers in this chapter are also short. Some are re-oriented attitudes rather than words. They can generally be said or offered in the space of one breath or less. They can be prayed many times in the course of a minute. They are small enough to go anywhere. Such prayers can be used quietly, in-teriorly, even in the midst of all my other daily activities and obligations. They can be integrated into my schedule, or used in special times set aside for prayer alone. The idea for me is to have a point of reference to keep coming back to, no matter what is transpiring outside or in.

The dangerous prayers that follow are drawn from my foundations in Christianity and my last twenty-six years with-in the Western Baul tradition as represented by my teacher.

Other traditions will offer you many additional choices for praying dangerously, and I strongly advise that you draw from your own tradition, since these are already deeply imbedded in your consciousness. I offer these brief meditations as examples of what it might mean to pray dangerously.

# 1. "Open My Heart, Open My Eyes"

"I want to be able to make prayer more a part of my daily life," she remarked.

"Do you read the papers?" I asked her. "Do you go to the supermarket regularly? Do you see and feel the pain that people are in?"

My friend wasn't prepared for the hard edge in my answer. She wanted a way to stay centered throughout the day, which commonly translates to "being undisturbed." I was asserting that praying dangerously, or bringing prayer into every moment of her life, would not be done without disturbance. Our intention to pray dangerously, which is essentially our willingness to be used for a purpose other than our own comfort and satisfaction, would have the effect of re-enlivening nerve endings long numbed, or melting the walls of ice and snow that we have shored up for protection around our heart. Slowly, inexorably, we start to notice more. We feel more. Transformation is occurring.

We can't pray, I mean really pray dangerously, unless we have our eyes open to reality. And reality as it is on the planet today is genuinely devastating, heartbreaking. The Buddha said it when he gave us the first noble truth: All life is suffering. Not just the life in the hospitals. Not just the life at the forefront of the war. Not just the life in the home where the couple are divorcing and using their children as ammunition in their hatred. No, all life. Period. Look at the smiles or the sultry frowns on the faces of the rich and famous. Look in their eyes. See suffering in the faces of billionaires, in the screen stars and rock idols, in the excruciating hunger for more possessions that drives shoppers to the world's largest mall. No one escapes it. No one.

Our hearts must be broken open, otherwise our prayer remains surface, superficial. We must be willing to go into hell—the hells both public and private—that lurk around every corner, including the corners of our own home. There is suffering. No right, wrong, good or bad about it. Suffering is. Humanity incarnated means that suffering is.

When the heart is truly broken open it will cry and that cry is the beginning of prayer, genuine prayer, but dangerous. I don't mean when the heart is washed with a wave of feeling sad or guilty because there are poor starving babies in the city. That's nothing. As soon as that wave recedes we can run and put up a buffer of some sort to keep the next one from reaching our beach blanket. We can distract ourselves with some activity or some transcendent thought, even with prayer. We pray for these poor suffering others, failing to see that we are suffering too.

Only when the heart is truly broken will we know compassion. We will know that those suffering others are not other than ourselves, as close as our own children, as needy and desperate as we are. We then are no longer praying *for* someone, as if we were separate from them. When we know ourselves in and with others, not separate from all that is, our prayer becomes communion—not an imploring of some great being beyond us to somehow intervene and make things better, but a conversation of the heart between sisters and brothers, or between lovers; a conversation that often has and needs no words. Our prayer becomes love, and love is not cool, undisturbed or safe.

How do you make prayer more a part of everyday life? Well, you can certainly program in ways to do it, and we have considered this in another place. But most of all you start to make prayer a part of life by opening your own eyes, seeing what is out there without turning away and especially without overlaying some spiritualized explanation for what you see. You open your eyes in your own home and in your own neighborhood, and in your own bedroom when you are alone and feeling afraid of your death. You don't run away from yourself or others. Rather, you let yourself be broken a little more, you let yourself die a little more, you let yourself feel the pain of creation in the profound labor of birthing itself. But, and here's the challenging part, you don't get swept into the indulgence of suffering. You don't make judgements or analyses about the suffering. You just look. You just feel. You don't obsess about your own suffering. You don't become so depressed by what you see that you lose your objectivity. Praying dangerously means that you simply let your heart be broken open, nothing more. It's no big deal.

> He who would save himself lives bare and calm,
> He who would save the world must share its pain.
> —Sri Aurobindo, from *Savitri*

How easy it is to get the idea that we are somehow doing well in our spiritual life when things are working for us, when things are hanging together rather than falling apart. Yet, this very falling apart is the stuff of most of life. And, when we can let ourselves fall apart we can also stay soft, flexible, open, compassionate.

I was asked to speak about prayer to a small group of friends one night. A woman told me that gratitude was her constant prayer, and I was impressed. But, as she went on, I realized that her gratitude was actually a defense against life. "I am so grateful for the sunshine, for the flowers, for the blessings of health, for my wonderful family ..." her list went on.

"Do you express gratitude for the storms, for the illness, for the down times too?" I asked her. The look on her face told me that this was an entirely foreign concept to her. Amazingly, she had reached sixty years of age without the recognition that it all came as gift from God. She was still protecting herself against the bad things by trying to be extremely grateful for the good things.

"When we are in the midst of the 'bad' things," I remarked, unaware of exactly how this point was going to be made, "we should actually be praying, 'Knock me down harder, Lord.'" I surprised myself with the words. They had come from a place deeper than the mind. Those words surprised another man in the group. "Please say more about that," he inquired in earnest, aware that these words held some potential for contemplation.

"'Knock me down harder, Lord,' is an appeal that can't come from the rational mind," I told him, relying upon the inner guidance of my teacher in that moment, since such a prayer was much too scary for me to suggest to someone else. "The idea is that such set-backs can be invaluable interventions into our rigidified programs for holiness or happiness. The hard knocks are actually wake-up calls that keep us aware and listening. And, it is possible to run *toward* such knocks rather than away from them, once we glimpse the possibility for compassion and service that comes when we are off our high horse. It is possible to stay open in the midst of breakdown, or 'to keep the heart open in hell,' as author Stephen Levine has described, and even to ask for more. It is possible to participate in a larger arena of humanity's suffering, using our prayer as a means of transforming suffering into the substance of love."

There wasn't anything more I could say in that moment. The group sat silently, as I did.

When we pray to see, to have our eyes open, to experience life in *all* its textures, we are rendering a request to God, to the universe, asking to fully participate in life. With eyes opened we are guided to celebrate everything, joyful or heartbreaking.

## 2. "SHOW ME TRUTH"

It is dangerous to see what is true in the labyrinth of illusions in which we generally slough around. Sure, we might think it would be great to know and live the truth, but do we *really* want it? Do we really want to know how bad things are, and how good things are? Words are cheap, of course. How often we run for cover at the first glimpse of life as it actually is.

On one hand: Have you ever asked anybody for feedback about your behavior in a situation, and then, as soon as they started, you immediately defended yourself or made them wrong for bringing up such a mean interpretation, while you secretly hoped they'd choke in mid-sentence? I think prayer is difficult and dangerous for much the same reason. Our prayer exposes us to truth, and to deeper and more refined levels of what is true, what is real, all the time. And such exposure is not without its price and its responsibility.

On the other hand: Our prayer might reveal the truth of our essence as infinite potential, "basic goodness,"[1] pure love, "organic innocence."[2] Now, *that* recognition might be more terrifying to bear than any negative feedback. The force of such love, such goodness, is annihilating to the separative self.

Or from another perspective altogether: If you lived in a protected palace, much like Prince Siddhartha did, and had been shielded from the vision of aging, disease and death, imagine the shock, the challenge, the burning question, when you first saw evidence of human suffering.

What if you, like the Buddha Siddhartha, suddenly realized that the whole world that you'd invested in was no more than a lovely theatrical stage meant to distract you from true life. What then? Would you, like Jim Carey in "The Truman Show," have the courage to walk off the set, or like Keanu

Reeves in "The Matrix," swallow the blue pill? Would you have to quit your job? Leave your husband or wife? Move to a Pacific island and attend to lepers? Or worse, would you have to unplug your TV; go out of your way to pick up your neighbor; speak more gently to your child?

It is dangerous to pray. It is dangerous to ask to see the multiple ways and means by which we establish separation—the big illusion—and dangerous to see the unflagging struggle we maintain to keep our separation-illusion fed. "I am *not* ...," we protest. "I am *not* inseparable from the One ... I am not the beloved of Christ ... I do not have Budhha nature. I am *not* interconnected with all life." It is dangerous to see such truth because once we've seen behind the curtain it will take a lot more denial and distraction to keep this recognition, and its hounding responsibility, at bay. Once we wake up, even for a moment, to the truth of who we are and how it all fits together with the pain that is obviously around us, it is extremely difficult and more uncomfortable than ever to go back to sleep again.

The Fourth Way teacher, E.J. Gold, in his book *The Joy Of Sacrifice*, writes about nineteen sacrifices that serve as markers of the spiritual journey.[3] The first sacrifice—to which he assigns the number "0"—is the sacrifice of peace of mind. "Wait a minute," you might be saying, "isn't peace of mind one of the main aims of the spiritual path? Is he suggesting that we end the quest before we even begin it?" When I first heard about this sacrifice I had much the same reaction. I didn't understand it. In fact, I recoiled from the words. Instead of simply observing the discomfort of what I was feeling as a result of those words, I plunged into debate, objecting to what I made up about what Mr. Gold was saying.

Reading further, however, I found that Gold was asserting something different. As he explains it, this first sacrifice "is brought about simply by being exposed to the possibility of knowledge, thus having the opportunity for transformation."[4] He means that once we hear the truth, or as he says "knowledge," we are disturbed forevermore. Such an intrusion upsets our well-arranged apple cart. We can never again rest in the bliss of unconscious distraction the way we may have allowed ourselves in the past. We might try to go off and devote our lives to nothing but fun and frolic, but always, around every corner, it will be there, this remembrance of things seen.

Genuine prayer has much the same effect. Once the face of God is glimpsed (I speak poetically here), once the possibility of life-surrendered is shown to us, we are like people chased by a posse from which we can never escape. In time, what has been begun in us will flower, if we only give it the attention it needs; and even a minimal amount of water and pruning will have enormous effects in this garden. In the experience of people who pray, the idea that God takes ten steps toward us for every one we take toward God is a tangible reality. Said another way, even the smallest opening of the heart allows the flow of Divine grace or benediction to circulate. Once the circulation starts, the very force of that grace will widen the crack. Pretty soon, the door is wide open.

There is another way to read Gold's words too. (The Sufis often say that there are seven levels of truth and that by meditating on certain stories or examples one will eventually drop into new and deeper understandings.) One could read them in much the way I did when I first heard them, as if he was asking us to give up the very peace of mind that we were looking for in the spiritual life, a recommendation that my own teacher has made to his students repeatedly.

Most of us have such preconceptions about what peace is, and more likely than not, since we are products of an overstressed culture, such peace is often equated with a certain lack of tension and lack of responsibility. Our imaginations about enlightenment generally fall into the same category. We somehow think that this exalted state means that we never have to get our hands dirty again. When, quite the contrary, the great souls who manifest this state most profoundly are those who are sweating blood, working tirelessly for others. So it is that the Fourth Way master might suggest that everything, including all notions about peace of mind, must be sacrificed in order to make room for what is ultimately real. Gold's words are giving us a jump-start in this domain of prayer. Namely, we can't pray if we are not willing to "give it up"… the "it" being whatever we cling to for security, permanence and our definitions of peace.

To pray dangerously, then, is to willingly expose ourselves to the undoing of our illusions, and to the disruption of our polite and highly-controlled means of existence. It is to throw ourselves voluntarily into the arena. It is to lay down our peace of mind, so that our hunger for truth can grow. It is to lay down our peace of mind, because the peace we have achieved has been a false one. It is to lay ourselves open to the chaos so that the chaos may be redeemed, or blessed.

Grasping after peace of mind, like grasping after comfort, is the surest way to discourage it. Prayer is dangerous because it undoes everything.

## BODHI

Some days are like this,
you wake with an ache in your chest
that isn't even yours.
You know that somewhere, great rivers
   of blood are being shed.
Somewhere, mothers are weeping over
   children, bodies strewn like wildflowers.
Somewhere, men and women eat a bowl of pain—
A man tells his wife that he is leaving,
A woman wakes in an empty bed
or puts her hand to an empty place
   where a breast was.
Somewhere, in the screeching of brakes
   there is a shattering, of glass, of lives.

This earth is covered in a sea of suffering.
If for a few moments we manage to forget
   do not begrudge us our wine, our prayer, our reaching out
for a word, a touch,

even from a stranger.

—RSR

## 3. "Others First"

An anonymous poem that I still remember from childhood is actually a most dangerous prayer, despite its trite, sing-song rhythm:

Lord, help me live from day to day
In such a self-forgetful way
That even when I kneel to pray
My prayer may be for others.
"Others, Lord, yes, others."
Let this my motto be.
Help me to live for others
That I may live like Thee.

Such prayers actually wreck plans for power, success, prestige and accomplishment. Yet still, many of us pray them; we say we want this.

A few years ago I watched a video of a commemorative funeral service for contemporary Zen master Maezumi Roshi. Amidst all the tributes, one in particular stood out. One of his peers reported that Roshi had, early on in his life of practice, taken on the commitment of putting others first. That tribute hit me hard.

Ever try to put others first for a whole day? How about for the length of a single meal? In my spiritual community we often receive boxes of day-old baked goods, the gift of a member who runs a coffee shop. If one happens to be sitting at the end of the table, one knows that their choice of treats will rarely be the fluffiest croissants or the chocolate-filled pastries, which are always taken first. On the occasion when I happen to be sitting near the head of the table, I too will covet the croissant, especially the chocolate one. No doubt about it, I'll grab it! Such are the habits of survival. "Others first" is a great prayer in principle, but in the midst of the battle? Hey, it's every woman for herself. Or maybe not. Just maybe, our joy might be to sacrifice our own preferences to bring joy to those around us, and to make that sacrifice invisibly: "No thanks, no croissant today, I've been *dreaming* of bran muffins!" Certainly caring parents do that all the time. Literally, mothers will starve to let their children eat. Fathers will give up their lives for their kids to live.

A life of prayer holds the potential to highlight the needs of others to the point where we genuinely want to serve them more than we want to preserve ourselves. We serve not because we'll get some points for the service, not because we'll get noticed for being generous, but simply because such service becomes the form of our lovemaking. We almost have no choice anymore, as anything less selfless is dry and lifeless. We treasure the communion it offers—a communion with humanity, and an intimate communion with God.

My teacher liked to make warnings of the dire consequences of involvement in spiritual life. He dramatically discouraged the merely curious, urging them to run in the opposite direction, telling them that this work would invade every corner of their world, leaving no room for their own hobbies and amusements. Most people laughed, thinking he was just making such declarations to make spiritual work sound even more special—like membership in some exclusive club.

He wasn't joking. My teacher meant it. He had no life of his own and knew the price of life surrendered to others—the price to ego; the price to the survival-based self that wants to preserve its privacy, its territory, its comfort. And yet, he had no choice. He wouldn't have used those words, because he wouldn't speak about himself this way, but I'll say it without apology, his love did such things. His only good pleasure was that others find liberation, love, the heart of God.

The Indian spiritual master, Swami Prajnanpad, who died in 1974, left his disciples a simple gauge of the spiritual process. He pointed out four steps or four stages of the path. The first stage he called "Self only," the second "Self and others," the third "Others and self," the fourth, simply "Others."

This four-step overview has long been useful to me as I've observed my own journey. Almost everyone starts out on the path of spirituality or the path of prayer with primary concern for "self." We are infants, growing into adolescence, evolving to adults and hopefully to wise elders, even if it takes lifetimes. As beginners or infants then, we will naturally be concerned with survival issues. We want spiritual nourishment, and we will grasp for it. We want relief from suffering; we will trample whatever is in the way to getting it. Because we want others to like and approve of us, we often compromise the inclinations of our deep heart, and learn the sorry consequences of that. We feel an emptiness that wants to be filled; we take this sense of emptiness personally. Nothing wrong here, these are simply our starting points and our default programs. We'll return again and again to self above all else whenever we are up against the wall, unless grace intervenes.

As we maintain our course on this path, we won't be able to deny that others around us are also in such need and pain. Who can miss it? Because we have sensitive hearts, then, we expand our concern to embrace these others. Certainly we pray for ourselves, and cry out for our own relief, and also we more frequently remember that we are not alone in our grief. We add an addendum that includes the sufferings of others. At last, we are learning compassion. We can rejoice! Still, their sufferings remain secondary to our own, and if asked to choose between self and others, as much as we'd like to imagine greater altruism, we must admit that it's "me first." Only in telling this truth again and again, observing it in everything, will we ever evolve with it. Honesty is perhaps the only way to move the process forward. Honesty without self-deprecation or judgment, that is. If we heap revilement on our poor heads, we slow down the natural evolutionary potential. In the meantime, however, it hurts to admit how selfishly concerned I am. And, it takes enormous courage to sit with this pain without trying to sweeten it by "being good," to impress ourselves or others, as a strategy for achieving relief.

To *sit in our selfishness* doesn't mean that we have to indulge it, however. We don't have to build a shrine to self-concern and start practices around it, asking "Mirror mirror on the wall who is the fairest one of all?" Actually, if we are honestly practicing self observation we will see that while we are self-concerned and that this causes us enormous suffering, so also are others self-concerned, just trying to survive no matter what the cost. And some of these costs are horrifically large, terribly final, as those serving long prison sentences will testify. Honesty thus earns us entry into stage two: self and others. We can no longer imagine a merely comfortable and self-satisfied life. Rather, we long to share what we have. We want to give back. It is only a matter of time (although time may mean decades if not lifetimes) before the "wanting" starts to grow legs. The wanting evolves as it is backed up with the strengthening of the spinal cord of practice—with the yoga of consistency, with free choice to go against the grain in order to build courage, with the expression of kindness even when we don't feel like it, with small acts of generosity. Such persistence furthers. Slowly we cross the bridge from self and others, to others and self. It happens!

I have great faith in this process that has begun in me, in us. I therefore assume that most of my readers, like myself, are working on that bridge between stages two and three. That is, we are slowly being grown from the stage of "self first others second," to that of "others first and self second." I know this because I feel the longing for it. Even if I can't yet live full-time in the country of others first, I can make tiny sojourns into this lovely territory. I can take a picnic lunch across the bridge now and then. I can set my intention here, despite knowing that I may not recognize "myself" on that other side. Still, I want to serve others, as I want a life of prayer.

If this maturing on the spiritual path is what we want, and certainly we *say* it is, why are we wasting time in trying to preserve ourselves so thoroughly? Why are we working so hard to keep things safely under control? That's what we do, isn't it? What are we waiting for by hanging out in the vestibule of the temple for so long? Why aren't we encouraging our own evolution in this process, this life of the spirit, in any way we can, leaving the results to God? Why aren't we praying dangerously?

The poet Dorothy Walters sums up the challenge at hand in her poem, "The Task":[5]

This is like a lover
who gives no rest
but demands, and demands, and demands.

Do you think this is a time for pausing,
for lying about under the pine trees
sampling your lunch pail?

If you are chosen to be the consort,

do not refuse the King.
If you have been outfitted
for a journey to the Himalayas,
do not nibble away your provisions
before you reach the ice.

## The Buddhist Prayer—Gaining Merit for Others

As a Catholic child I learned my prayers well. I was to forgive my enemies as I hoped to be forgiven by God. I was instructed even to *love* my enemies, to do good to those who hurt me, and to pray for those who persecuted me. The way I internalized those profound teachings, however, was generally with the sense that my enemies were some bad guys out there, and I was being the good guy in praying for them. They might persecute me, sure, but because I was a Christian I would show them a thing or two. I'd turn the other cheek!

Of course, this was a childish interpretation of this teaching, but the traces of this approach to prayer for others lasted long into my adult years. Ultimately, this view was matured. But it was not only through the profound examples of Catholic or Christian people that I heard and saw the inner teaching in this doctrine of "love your enemies" or "live for others." Through the witness of selflessness and compassion that I found in contemporary Buddhist men and women, particularly the Tibetan Buddhists, this more mature understanding of prayer for others was powerfully revealed for me.

Reading about the conditions of those Tibetans held in prisons and camps in China and Tibet, many of them Buddhist monks and nuns, I was often brought to tears with the sufferings that these brave men and women endured. But, what broke my heart, astounding all my sensibilities, was their witness of loving-kindness toward their captors.

Some who had been in prisons for over twenty years actually wept for the sad karmic predicament of their guards or government officials, who they believed would have to work and probably suffer, either in this lifetime or in future lifetimes, to balance the disharmony created by their actions. Others prayed for their "enemies" even while they were being tortured.

One story that moved me was told by Chagdud Tulku Rinpoche, a contemporary Tibetan teacher, about his sister, T'hrinlay Wangmo, who was beaten almost to the point of death by a Chinese official.

Prior to the incident, T'hrinlay's father had warned her that her hot tongue, directed toward the Chinese, would get her in trouble. Nonetheless she could not curb it, and on several occasions the Chinese had tried to kill her.

Once apprehended, and as T'hrinlay was being beaten, she was not angry at her attacker. In fact, she recognized the beating as karmic purification and prayed that her suffering might allow others to be spared. When her wounds healed almost immediately (an indication of her spiritual power), the official was so amazed that he invited her to stay at his house and gave her a large sum of money as she left, asking her to pray for him at the time of his death.

Sometime after the incident in question T'hrinlay Wangmo was passing through the city where this Chinese official worked. A funeral procession stopped her progress. Inquiring who the dead man was, she was told that it was the very man who had invoked her prayers after almost killing her. At that moment T'hrinlay Wangmo prayed for him, happy to be fulfilling the promise she had made.

This grace to think of others even in the midst of one's own pain may seem fantastic, or we might imagine that such compassion is shown only by a highly evolved soul. Yet, for those who are drawn to prayer, such selfless offerings are really not outside our realm of possibilities. At least we desire such selflessness, even if we don't always practice it. If we examine our own hearts, we find a longing for union, a desire to live beyond separation, because it is our most basic, real condition. We long to dissolve the illusion that we are separate from others and from everything else.

Practically, T'hrinlay Wangmo did not hold herself above her attacker, as better than him, hence she had no anger toward him. She evidently saw herself as inextricably bound to him and to others. In praying for others to be spared, and in praying for attacker, she was healing herself and fulfilling her dedication to a life of loving-kindness, the epitome of spiritual life.

We face similar challenges each in our own way, and daily perhaps. We face the choice of whether to act upon our desires for revenge and righteousness, or whether to rededicate our lives to the liberation of ourselves and others. There are only ever two choices—either we practice loving-kindness or we exert self-will. Like when Fed-Ex misplaces a package and I have to call and handle the situation. Will I treat the customer service rep with contempt or with kindness? When I have to wait on line in the grocery store and the person in front of me fumbles to find their credit card, or painstakingly writes out their check, will I generate impatience or loving-kindness? Is my life for myself or for them, after all? But, surely, one's ex-husband who regularly misses sending child support, surely he is worthy of disdain? No, here too one has a choice in how to act.

Prayer for others helps us to place the intention we wish to live for directly in front of us; it orients our attitude. Over time, such intentional prayer for others begins to stand up on its own legs, to permeate all our waking hours. We start to see the underlying condition of suffering in which all beings flounder. We see the interrelatedness of all lives—how our impatience affects those around us, even subtly. We connect to the vast ocean of being in which we all exist.

The following prayer, written by Chagdud Tulku, epitomizes dangerous prayer as we have been considering it. Here we are invited to completely surrender our lives for the benefit of others, dedicating not only all the good we are doing or will ever do, but making use of all that we have ever done in the past as well.

It is a prayer that could seriously change a life.

### Red Tara Dedication Prayer

Throughout my many lives and until this moment, whatever virtue I have accomplished, including the merit generated by this practice, and all that I will ever attain, this I offer for the welfare of sentient beings.

May sickness, war, famine, and suffering be decreased for every being, while their wisdom and compassion increase in this and every future life.

May I clearly perceive all experiences to be as insubstantial as the dream fabric of the night and instantly awaken to perceive the pure wisdom display in the arising of every phenomenon.

May I quickly attain enlightenment in order to work ceaselessly for the liberation of all sentient beings.

(In, *Red Tara: An Open Door to Bliss and Ultimate Awareness*. P.O. Box 279, Junction City, Calif., 96048: Padma Publishing, p. 10.)

## Praying for Others

Before she left for a two week retreat, Elinor anticipated this special time for herself. She was a zealous practitioner and saw the opportunity for more silence and solitude as the chance to go deeper, to work diligently with her mind, to enliven her devotion. As she spoke to me I was attuned to how much she sounded like me. Her focus, like mine, was on "my spiritual life" and "my practice." In short, she looked forward to an uninterrupted time to relax the strictures that kept her heart so guarded; a chance to really see what "she" was up to in her life, and thereby to reorient her priorities. Without the usual sources of comfort or consolation that she relied upon in her day to day life, she was thrilled to be able to plumb the depths of her heart and soul, to listen for the voice of the Beloved, as we've talked about here and elsewhere.

What was it that rubbed against the grain for me as she spoke? I wondered. All that she talked about was true. I'd had the same desires at the beginning of most of my own retreats. I venture to say that most earnest men and women of prayer can relate to her strong intentions. And yet?

Then I saw it, as familiar as my own face. I saw that as fine as such intentions were, they were still all about "me" or in this case all about Elinor and "her" insights, her process and ultimately, let's face it, "her" enlightenment. Still, despite my own misgivings about the orientation she planned, I knew it wasn't up to me to question her intentions. She was entering into prayer and silence to hear God's direction, and I trusted (well, as much as I could) that this intention would be rewarded in God's own good time, and in God's own good way. I hugged her and blessed her both in my heart and with my arms.

## A Work for Others

Two weeks later, as I joined Elinor for lunch at the conclusion of her retreat, she confirmed what my heart already knew. Her experience in seclusion was vastly different from the one she had planned.

"Soon after I entered my hut," she told me with blazing eyes, "I was met with the words of my friend Patricia who was in the midst of a painful separation from her husband. Patricia had asked, 'Please pray for me,' just before I came here." At the time, Elinor told me, Patricia's request had shocked her. The idea of praying *for* others was not a part of her usual repertoire. Not that she didn't appreciate the notion, but simply that for so many years she'd been occupied with her own need to *get something* from her practice, and particularly while on retreat. Surely she made many generic prayers, which included such grand intentions as world peace and the relief of suffering throughout the world, but Patricia and *her* needs as a focus of prayer, that was a different matter. In general, others (even intimate others) and *their* immediate needs were assigned a back seat.

As she entered into her two-week seclusion, Elinor was inspired to take this remembrance and request quite seriously. Despite feeling insecure, "like, just *how* do you pray for others?" she began like a beginner, making it up as she went along, the way a child might try on clothing that is too big just to have the delight of feeling grown up. As she prayed for her friend Patricia, Elinor soon found herself praying for Patricia's husband, and then for Patricia's daughter. And then, one thing naturally leading into another, she was praying "for" more and more people. "It was almost like they started lining up outside the door, begging for a connection to whatever it was that I was connecting with during this very sacred time.

They wanted blessing, mercy, healing, strength … love, and I was serving it up in generous measure from my little camp on the hillside."

The cumulative effect of praying for others genuinely surprised Elinor. She was unprepared for what it changed. "The whole focus of my experience was shifted," she said. "Miraculously, and much to my great relief, I was relieved of the burden, the huge weight, of self preoccupation. It was actually a weight I didn't realize I was carrying, at least with regard to the work of the spirit." Once that preoccupation was gone, a glorious spaciousness arose within and around her, she told me. When the needs of others became more central than her own, she honestly disappeared into the role of being "pray-er." Instead of being the one who is praying for others or for the world, she was actually simply the space in which prayer happened. She was the temple or the container, so to speak. Prayer arose, and the energy of that arising prayer attracted the needs and pleas of the world. That open spaciousness was itself a stronghold of blessing force, a chamber of purification, a healing spot, a stream of refreshment. Her openness to prayer was an oasis to which others were drawn. She was merged with the energetic field of the world, and was being used for the sake of others. Pray-er and pray-ee were not separate in the matrix in which she lived for this precious time. The individual who made the intention to serve others through prayer was consumed by something larger. Elinor had indeed started the ball rolling, but Love had caught it.

The poet Steven Spender once wrote, "The Spirit wants that there be flying. As to who or what does the flying, in that it has only a passing interest."

# 4. "Make Me an Instrument of Thy Peace"

Lord, make me an instrument of Your peace. Where there is hatred, let me sow love; where there is injury, pardon; where there is doubt, faith; where there is despair, hope; where there is darkness, light; where there is sadness, joy.

O Divine Master, grant that I may not so much seek to be consoled as to console; to be understood as to understand; to be loved as to love.

For it is in giving that we receive. It is in pardoning that we are pardoned. It is in dying that we are born to eternal life.

—Francis of Assisi

Lots of us identify with this idea of being used for God's work. There is something grand about the gesture, thinking of ourselves like a brush in the hands of Michaelangelo as he painted the ceiling of the Sistine Chapel, or a pen in the hand of St. John as he wrote his gospel of love. We might imagine that being an instrument of God's peace is a bit like being selected as an ambassador or an emissary to a foreign kingdom. When we pray such a prayer I wonder if there is ever a thought of bloodshed associated with it, or the possibility of raging heat and mosquitoes forever, or deep pain?

Are we really ready to be made into instruments so that we can be used? Do we really know what we are asking for? Think about it, how is an instrument made? For instance, how did a blacksmith make a great strong shovel or a samurai's sword? The blacksmith plunged the metal into the fire until it smoldered red hot. He removed it and let it cool slightly, resting it to just the right temperature. From the sword's perspective, it may have wondered if it was ever going to be anything but a sorry lump. Then, just when the metal had given up hope, the smith picked up his hammer and pounded it into shape, only to plunge the sword back into the fire a few minutes later. And again, and again.

Certainly this is the way to form a trustworthy instrument, one that will not crack when put to the test. One that will be whole. Is it any different with us, the human instruments? God's instruments need to be trustworthy. They will be molded to suit God's purposes by the challenges of their lives, but also by the self-initiated discipline of the practices they have embraced. God is not out to hurt us and make us suffer, neither was the blacksmith. God simply wants good instruments.

I have often been threatened with death. I have to say, as a Christian, that I don't believe in death without resurrection. If they kill me, I will rise again in the Salvadoran people. I tell you this without any boasting, with the greatest humility. As pastor, I am obliged by Divine command to give my life for those I love, who are all Salvadorans. Even for those who are going to assassinate me. If the threats are carried out, even now I offer my blood to God for the redemption and resurrection of El Salvador. Martyrdom is a grace of God I don't deserve. But if God accepts the sacrifice of my life, may my blood be the seed of liberty and the sign that hope may soon become reality. You may say, if they come and kill me, that I forgive those who did it. Hopefully they may realize that they will be wasting their time. A bishop will die, but the church of God, which is the people, will never perish.—Oscar Romero (*Salvadorean Archbishop Romero spoke these words on March 10, 1980. Fourteen days later he was killed by an assassin's bullet while saying Mass in a hospital chapel.)[7]

When we pray, "Lord, make me an instrument ..." we are asking not only to be used but to first be made into that instrument. It is always a dangerous prayer because it will cost us, and the self-protective mechanisms and the judgements of reason will cry out against such treatment: "It is not fair!"

We want to be transformed, but we also want to hold onto our own will, and it does not work this way. The instrument really doesn't have a choice, and herein lies the ecstasy of such surrender, that we are being used up for a purpose larger than ourselves. We are being given the opportunity to offer our lives back to the One from whom we received life in the first place.

It is only right.

May I be medicine for those who are sick, a partner for those who are lonely; a bridge for those who need to cross over, and a light for those who are blind.

—a prayer of the Bodhisattva

## 5. "Let it Burn"—Alchemical Prayer

The athanor was the alchemist's slow burning furnace. Any substance placed within it was heated to great intensity, causing its various elements to be cooked, either burned off or melded. The magician's intention was to create a new and more perfect substance.

The alchemist's work with the athanor is an appropriate metaphor of praying dangerously, as the process of prayer too is one of transformational possibility. In prayer, we take the raw stuff of our lives, chunky and impure though they be, and subject them to the heat that will purify and refine them, changing their composition, form and efficacy.

The athanor was a slow cooker, but reliable—the alchemist used coal for the heat source. In our prayer I find that love, intention and stillness are the best fuels, as they burn longest and thus provide the most potential for a new substance to be created. Our prayers rarely start out as liquid gold, as transcendental bliss. More often they start from a sense of desolation, when everything seems dry, dull, lacking in any purpose, let alone full of magic.

Perhaps we come to prayer because of a searing grief, like the loss of a beloved friend or family member; or out of remorse that we denied ourselves a chance to listen and thus to love someone who disagreed with us. Prayer may start with only a small glimmer of longing for dedication or devotion to something that is bigger than we are. Or it may emerge from a sense that we are being choked, strangled by our own hands and stuffed into a tiny box of fear. Any or all of these events may level us, causing us to fall to our knees at last. From here we may make a genuine cry to heaven. If we are lucky we may recognize the signs scratched on the inner walls of the athanor by the subjects of previous experiments. They say, "Welcome to the alchemical process of prayer." But the signs also say something a bit disconcerting. They caution: *Warning, You could die in here.*

And isn't that really what we've come to prayer for—to die? Praying within the athanor is dangerous because ultimately it means the death to all the versions of self that we've put stock in. It means death to all the illusions of what is currently going to bring me a happiness that will not quit, ever. It means death to relationships that don't feed the truest intentions of my soul, and jobs that don't serve the work of God on earth, and diversions that capture and contain me, keeping me distracted from my aim. And for this I should be enormously grateful. But am I?

In one of the poems of praise he wrote to his master, the Indian Beggar-saint Yogi Ramsuratkumar, my teacher Lee Lozowick composed a most dangerous prayer which says, in part:

Crush all illusion in us, all that is not You and Yours,
shatter all false ideas,
dispel all projections and expectations,
    leaving only Your Name,
Yogi Ramsuratkumar, Yogi Ramsuratkumar,
    and resurrecting on the grave
of our hypocrisies and our self-centeredness
    Praise, Sweet Praise of You,
our Lord, Father, Savior and Adored.[8]

Many other wise mentors have described this process of alchemical transformation out of which prayer, praise and adoration may arise. Personally, instead of "crushing" I resonate more strongly with any analogy to a "slow burn" because my prayer and my inner experience tends to be hot, and therefore somewhat explosive. But explosive fires don't necessarily do the work that is needed. Instead, they may merely incinerate rather than purify and cook.

One of the reasons I appreciate my retreat practice (two to three weeks each year in which I do nothing but allow love, intention and stillness to reign) is that I can't go anyplace or do anything progressive with my creative inspirations. Alone in my hermitage I am washed with waves of creativity. Ideas for new books and new poems and new projects to enact with the children in my life arise every time I sit down in the silence; plans pour forth for new workshops, for delightful surprises to offer my loved ones, for ways to redecorate my house once I get out.

And that's always the sticking point, this "when I get out." Often, this awareness of my focus on some imaginary "out there" shocks me into awakeness as I start to ask myself, "And what about right now?" How ready I am to miss this day, this moment even, because all of this energy is building for some colossal orgasm at the end of retreat.

When I can tap into this desire to express and to give while at the same time knowing that I'm not going anyplace, I often feel frustrated, unsettled. That's when I think about men and women in prisons all over the world. Millions of them! I open to the excruciating pain that these brothers and sisters must endure in their desire to *do* something—to serve or work in a way that will enrich their souls and express love, even while living in an environment that feeds self-hatred and violence to others. The sadness and loneliness of that life breaks me. Certainly I know that many have transcended terrible circumstances to become stars of light and inspiration, but just like every blind man is no Stevie Wonder, neither is every imprisoned person a Nelson Mandela or a Corrie Ten Boom.

In my own case I become filled and exhilarated, almost to bursting, with the raging storm of creativity and desire to serve. To try to stifle it would be foolish, I know. It is God's own life force racing through my veins. I'm enlivened by this energy. It thrills me. And, the *what's so* of retreat practice is that I'm not going anywhere. I will use no phone call to share my ideas with a friend and to plan the next step. I'll write no emails or make no postings to Facebook in which to announce my latest brilliant insights, and this is a good thing, as there is no easier way to spoil a good cake than to open the oven when it's rising. One of the most helpful bits of advice that others have given me in my spiritual journey has been to simply "let it burn." Such patience and trust can yield a result more wonderful than anything expected. I pass that wisdom on to you: Trust the alchemical process.

To let something burn is not to cover it and forget about it, which merely deprives a fire of the oxygen it needs to grow. No, especially when letting something burn I need to practice greater vigilance than ever, vigilance to assure that my mixture doesn't simply flare up and then die out, vigilance to guard the hearth, lest sparks ignite the nearby brush or dry roots. I am being taught (from within) what it means to take my own seat in the middle of these seething fires (or even just among a few smoldering coals) and to bow down here, and to wait. I can hold hot coals. I can love them and what they stand for without *doing anything* about them. I can offer them as gifts of light and warmth to the deity who reigns in my own heart. "Here," I can say, "You can take it, bake it, shake it out…while I'm simply going to breathe my way through this," sort of the way I might keep my mind focused during a root canal surgery. I can just hold still.

# 6. "THY WILL BE DONE"

"Whatever the will of our Father in heaven has for us
that is where my heart lies."
                    —a contemporary marriage vow

I first heard these words at a marriage ceremony enacted by
friends who are members of my spiritual community. These
words stay with me. I pray them frequently.

Such a marriage vow is extremely dangerous. Partners to
such a union should shake with holy dread at the implications
of it. Imagine the consequences of making such declarations
in a public setting—before one's teacher, or a minister of the
faithful who stands in the place of God, and before one's peers,
who represent the body of humanity. A man and a woman are
declaring not only that they wish to surrender to a will other
than their own; but further, that their hearts are in it.

How long will it take a husband or wife to forget the words
of their sacred vows? A few weeks, a few days, a few hours?
When the motivating hormones of the romantic stage of a
relationship are only a vague trace in the body, will a couple
remember that their lives are not their own to manage; that
their lives have been given away, entrusted to one another
and to God? Probably not. Nonetheless, the words they have
spoken remain as an objective testimony to the possibility of
transformation. They have prayed the most serious prayer that
any human being can ever pray. Even when they forget for
the 49,000th time, the vow still stands. It can be re-invoked,
recommitted.

"Thy will be done" is a phrase from the Christian "Lord's
Prayer," recited millions of times daily throughout the world—
at breakfasts for athletes preparing for the big game, at funeral

services for departed relatives, by children kneeling at the bedside. Does anybody *really* mean, "Thy Will Be Done"? Or are we all liars ... or unconscious hypocrites at best?

I don't offer this indictment to Christians only, certainly. The other great religious traditions of the world have similar orientations in their prayers. We find it in the Psalms, in the Koran, in the Bhagavad-Gita ... everywhere. Humanity prays "Thy will be done," but Jack and Carlita and Akash and Sara and Mei Mei don't want the will of God, unless of course it happens to coincide with their own desires for comfort, or pleasure, or victory, or retrieval from the jaws of death. We don't want the will of God if it means changing our lifestyle, or especially if it means swallowing our pride, or sharing our money, or getting wrinkled and flabby.

Without knowing what the will of God is in your case I can still say that you probably don't want it! How do I know? Because I know myself enough to know that I resist life in all its messy implications. I resist the weather, the traffic jam, the annoying habits of the guy I work with. I resist extending myself to others. I resist what I know needs to be done.

Would it, in fact, be better off to forget such prayers, as they are such arrogant protestations? Perhaps. Would it be better to stop saying, "We want peace," while we arm ourselves to the teeth and prepare for war? Would it be better to stop saying that we love our children when we abuse them by our neglect, assigning them to the programming of the television media? Such questions are not asked casually. The answers to such questions are not for the fainthearted.

Will we, individually, or as partners in a marriage, or as friends, or as members of the same community, or as citizens of a nation, be up to reaffirming this prayer, "Thy will be done," day in and day out, with one another? When times get tough?

When the boredom starts to set in? When there is sickness and a twist of fate? Suppose that a couple made it their ongoing inquiry with one another to discern the will of God, and then to follow it in their regard within the marriage. What if *that* became the topic of conversation at breakfast rather than the local or national news? This willingness to ask the question, "What is the will of God for me?" or "for us?"—a question to which there is no secure answer—is to plunge into exploration into God. But, what else are we really here for?

The will of God is no mystery, however. God is communicating constantly, we simply need to learn God's language so that we can hear the day's orders clearly. One learns God's language by watching and listening, and hanging out in God's culture. One observes the obvious. What is obviously needed in any situation, and what is in accordance with one's duties and responsibilities? That is the will of God. There it is, written in gigantic letters across the Hollywood Hills.

As Jean-Pierre Caussade, a seventeenth-century French priest, and author of the spiritual classic, *Abandonment to Divine Providence,* states: "You are seeking for secret ways of belonging to God, but there is only one: making use of whatever God offers you."[9]

Over the years I have learned that there are big clues to the discernment of God's will. First, that the will of God is found only in the present moment. Second, that the will of God is not hidden inside of events, like some difficulty that has a core of gold. God is not trying to hide the path from us. Third, that what is obviously wanted and needed in terms of service in the moment is an indicator of God's will. And fourth, that our current duties to and responsibilities for others, the requirements of our state of life, even if they were originally motivated by our egoic attachments of the past, are part and parcel of God's will for us now.

Insofar as we are able to stay attentive to the moment, we can serve the will of God. Insofar as we are able to abandon our ideas about what should happen, and what *we* demand to happen, and allow the situation as it is to reveal itself to us, we are amenable to discerning the will of God. "Thy will be done" is a prayer that will force us into this present moment, if we pray it from the heart.

## In God's Own Good Time

An adjunct consideration to praying for the will of God to be done is that of the timing involved. Without undermining the need for our participation and our practice, let's face it, the grace of God does it all—everything. And it does it all "in God's own good time," a phrase that I've come to love and count on.

The reality of "in God's own good time" as opposed to my timing causes frustration in me sometimes. It can be especially hard for the more impatient types, the spiritual racehorses who want some kind of dramatic results, or prizes for their prayers. Yet, I find the phrase provides a tremendous relief to the ardent seeker in me, and is actually an invitation to greater faith and radical reliance on God. This phrase itself is a dangerous prayer.

What am I impatient for anyway? For relief? For realization? For something more, or different, from what I already have? This moment, exactly as it is, is the doorway into God's room; this moment is the gate of eternity.

The appreciation of "in God's own good time" in the process of transformation is analogous to the timing involved in expert winemaking. Love is a great winemaker and we are the grapes, which get pressed by circumstance and experience.

With this pressing, our juice gets bottled. In our bottles, we wait on the cellar shelves, longing for ripeness, longing to be poured out, emptied; longing for this sense of completeness to fulfill the purpose of our existence. Yet, Love will serve no wine before its time. So, Love will keep the wine, allowing it to ferment to just the right degree before serving it.

How does this grape juice know exactly what the wine-maker is looking for in taste anyway? It doesn't. It can't. And what can the juice do to hurry along the process of its own ripeness? Nothing. It can do nothing but stay in place and wait. How ludicrous to think of the juice trying to swirl itself into a tempest in its bottle, trying to pop its own cork. The juice's job is to make no sudden moves.

And what does it mean to those of us who desire trans-formation into the heart of God that we must wait and make no sudden moves? It means that we do what is right in front of us, day in and day out, simply and quietly; it means that we keep to our daily practice of prayer, or other spiritual exercises as directed by our tradition or our teach-er; it means that we exhibit kindness in all our interactions insofar as we are able, and so on. It means that we allow and even celebrate the winemaster's timing, as different as it is from our own. The fermenting wine needs no will of its own. Things would go a lot easier if the grape juice would simply stop all its stupid maneuverings and just surrender to being wine-in-the-making, the subject of the master's timing, the master's will.

The wine will become ripe, if given the right care, the right conditions. Alchemical transformation will be true of us with-out our having to know anything about alchemical symbols or esoteric lore.

Surrendering to God's timing, as we noted earlier in the

book when we considered Radical Reliance on God, can become a constant form of daily prayer. If I watch myself carefully I note how frequently I attempt to impose my schedule upon the event at hand, rather than giving the event back to God and then listening for the inherent rhythm of the thing. Sometimes I want to speed up something that should be done slowly. Sometimes I want to slow down something that should be engaged vigorously. With intention and attention, such attunement does become more and more obvious over time. Although here again, the timing is God's. We simply practice in place.

As we attempt to practice alignment with God's timing, as in everything else, we can turn over all our efforts to God. Then, regardless of whether we directly sense any particular direction, any particular rhythm, or not, we can move forward anyway, taking our best guess and leaving the results to God.

# 7. "Thank God" —The Prayer of Gratitude

Gratitude grows quietly, often in the shadows of life's events. Sometimes we don't realize it is there until we get turned around, or until someone points it out to us. At other times gratitude blazes upon us, unmistakable, as when the sun suddenly emerges from behind the cloud bank. Once we have tasted gratitude, felt it in our cells, we have a point of reference for it, a point we can return to even when the sun disappears again.

Gratitude surprises the prisoner in his cell and the mother nursing her child. Gratitude happens to us in the midst of a great meal and as we undergo radiation treatment for cancer. The bird that hops across our path when we least expect it surprises us into re-alignment with the unfolding of nature all around us, suddenly calling us out of our self-obsession. Ah, blessed day!

When gratitude strikes, something wondrous fills us—a literal food-substance is injected into the soul. Unfortunately, we frequently choke that source off all too quickly because we start to bring the rational and analytic mind to bear on the situation, and thereby lose the wordless reality of gratitude. As soon as we try to grasp and hold it, it tends to take flight. Like love, we strangle gratitude when we try to make it our own private possession.

We may think that we have to immediately *do something* about the gratitude that spontaneously arises in us. We think that we have to write a thank-you letter, for instance. And in that very act we are often squashing our gratitude. No longer is the experience gratuitous, meaning free and unmerited. (The word gratitude comes from the Latin "gratia," meaning grace). All of a sudden our gratitude has a price tag—and we feel obliged to express it in some specific form.

Another reason we turn logical with our gratitude is that it is terrifying. The wonder of a moment in which there is nothing but an upwelling of simple happiness is utterly awesome. Gratitude is so close to the bone of life, pure and true, that it instantly stops the rational mind, and all its planning and plotting. That kind of let go is fiercely threatening. I mean, where might such gratitude end?

Let's look at gratitude another way. When we say that one is ungrateful what are we saying? Certainly we are not simply saying that he or she didn't say thank you for something. Rather, we are more likely saying that he or she is unaware, self-obsessed and so myopic that they are violating beautiful gifts, and refusing other gifts. We are saying that he or she is out of alignment with a certain law of reciprocity inherent in existence. The ungrateful will squander resources. The ungrateful will rampantly consume because they have not tasted what is already present to them. The ungrateful will continue to crave other experiences and things because he or she has not seen or felt what is.

It is hard to feel gratitude when we have our expectations already lined up. When our Christmas wish-list is set in stone we are going to be sadly disappointed when we don't receive what we've asked for. It is also difficult to feel gratitude when one is trying to control life, or trying to make success happen, either their own or someone else's.

These descriptions of ungratefulness don't just apply to those faceless, nameless others who are destroying everything. Ungratefulness is not simply the sin of the other guy. Each of us in our way is ungrateful, not because we don't say thanks but because our lives demonstrate that we have failed to see what is. If indeed we saw, we would naturally be grateful. If indeed we saw, we would pray.

The attitude of the spiritual renunciate or beggar—
exemplified by Francis of Assisi in the Western world, and
innumerable saints, monks and sadhus of India and the Far
East—is ideally one of enormous gratitude. Such a one takes
everything as gift and grace. Even misfortunes are cause for
gratitude, as the person undergoing the misfortune is drawn
into more radical awareness of life as it is, or into identification with the sufferings of others.

My teacher, Lee Lozowick, has gone so far as to equate
prayer with gratitude:

When we are living here and now, when we are accept-
ing what is, then every thought and every gesture is a
prayer. The way I define prayer it would be worship,
or an expression of gratitude in praise of God, wonderful and holy, magnificent, rather than some kind of
request — "Something for me, to make my life better,"
or even to make other people's lives better. That's supplication. When we understand that whatever arises
in the moment is the Gift of God, then we can praise
God for whatever is given. Life is the Gift of God, but
we don't know that, because we keep trying to mold
it in our image. And even that is something to be accepted as it is ... So, when we recognize that, there is
a sense of gratitude. And that may manifest as praise,
as service, or as complaint — strange as that seems.
But it's all prayer, because it rests in the context of the
recognition of what is as it is. The Universe is absolute,
so in the recognition of absoluteness, there is gratitude.
We don't have to say the words, "Thank you, God." All
we have to do is *live* here and now. Whatever action is
here and now as it is, is prayer.[10]

What will allow us to see or live life as it is, here and now? What will loosen the soil of our psyches and our bodies enough that we are able to be radically surprised? This is no small question. Actually it is a bit like asking what will ultimately transform us.

Unfortunately, for many of us that loosening will only happen when we are shocked by loss. On the other hand, we undertake spiritual practice consciously as an antidote to the cultural trance of ingratitude in which we are immersed. Meditation, prayer, awareness of breath, study of spiritual teachings, remembrance of Divine Presence, self-observation, the surrender of our own will, alignment with a spiritual teacher—these are the small daily shocks that will allow us to see. Each of these practices will cause the heart to open enough so that awareness of what is will flood us. To live in openness, in not-knowing, in the empty space of whatever *is*, that is what keeps us in the domain of gratitude.

When gratitude is not too swiftly expressed, but rather is allowed to burn within, it becomes an urgent fire that drives us forward. We are moved to serve, simply because we want to give back in the measure with which we have been blessed.

## Praise and Prayer

"Don't tell me what you believe or what your dogmas are. Tell me first *what you praise* and *how you praise*."
—Matthew Fox[11]

"Praising God … we come to know Him better.
Knowing Him better we love Him better,
loving Him better we find our happiness in Him."
—Thomas Merton[12]

More than three thousand years ago, the Israelite King David composed over one-hundred-fifty songs, which we know today as the psalms. These raw and exalted expressions of David's overwhelming amazement at the goodness of the Lord, these cries for help resounding from the depths of his soul, are a legacy that has endured to this day as a basis of ritual and prayer in both Judaism and Christianity.

While the psalms cover the full range of human emotions, from remorse to the desire for retribution, their overarching theme is singular—namely, the praise of God. With "shouts of joy and gladness," with proclamations of faith before the assemblies of nations, with "a new song of hope," with the repetition of mantric refrains—like, "His love is eternal!" (psalms 107, 118, 136) or "His mercy endures forever!" (repeated 26 times in psalm 136)—the psalmist addressed his Beloved. "From the rising of the sun until its going down" (psalm 113), David witnessed to the possibility of keeping the Lord's greatness, the Lord's name, uppermost in his awareness, by the act of praise.

Praise, in general, is a cheap commodity today. When luxuriant accolades are used to sell soap and beer and mouthwash, to create the images of Hollywood stars and football players, and to enhance self-esteem based on illusions, praise has become empty. Men and women today, even those who undertake some spiritual practice, may have turned their backs on the prayer forms of their childhood religions, and may, therefore, have few relevant models of genuine praise as genuine prayer. It may take some curiosity and intention to renew or establish praise as a form of prayer today.

Imagine how blessed it would be to live with a finely-tuned attention to beauty, and then to "offer" everything

beautiful—every lovely flower, landscape, child's face; everything pleasurable to taste; every sweet sound; every gesture of
elegance—to God, as an act of praise and thanksgiving. This
practice, along with many other forms for the expression of
praise and gratitude can be found in most spiritual traditions.
We humans praise the sacred with the voice through wondrous songs, poems, chants and litanies, and with the body by
dance, movement, music and art. When done with conscious
attention, rather than as "practices" to get through, these many
vocal, kinesthetic, musical forms offer a dynamic alternative to
the dead "praise" of contemporary culture. They give us a way
of praising that is grounded in the sacred, full of human passion, longing and raw nerve.

Down through the ages, the prophets and saints have made
the same cry: "Pray always!" "Praise him to the highest heavens." "Take the name of Hari." Praise endures as a universal
medium, apparently because praise works in transforming the
mundane into the sacred. It is time, I think, to renew a revolution in the understanding and appreciation of the prayer of
praise as a means of communing with God.

For those who were fortunate enough to have met a saint
or person of recognized holiness during his or her physical
life, such a meeting is not easily forgotten. In person, such
a one has a blessing force as tangible as a block of wood or
a slab of stone. Even after decades, people who saw Yogi
Ramsuratkumar, my teacher's guru, even only once, have told
me that they still remember the wonder, joy, and power they
felt in his presence. They still feel gratitude to him. This remembrance is all I need to initiate praise.

Once begun, praise tends to fuel itself. To "sing to the
Lord a joyful song" (psalm 95), as the psalmist David pro-
claims, can create joy in the heart and limbs of the singer. It is

very difficult to maintain a condition of isolation and tension when hands are being clapped, cymbals clanged, "Hosannahs" or "Jaya Guruayas" intoned. Yogi Ramsuratkumar asked again and again for "praise, more praise" because he knew that praising God brought God alive in our bodies. After all, his master, Swami Papa Ramdas had instructed him in this same reality. To speak the mantra, "Om Sri Ram Jai Ram Jai Jai Ram" was to awaken the Divine sleeping within the human heart.

> "When you take the Name, you are taking the Name of the Lord who dwells in your own heart."[13]
>
> —Papa Ramdas

### Who Needs It?

Does God *need* our praise? Probably not. At least not in any absolute sense. Do *we* need to praise God in everything in order to experience the fullness of life? Yes! The unfathomable and loving God, whom we mystics-in-training know (in brief glimpses at least) as not separate from ourselves, seems intent on sharing Itself. God therefore urges us to praise the Source of All, again and again, in order that we may participate in the song of gratitude that God sings to Itself and to creation throughout eternity. Therefore, as St. Augustine said, we should "Let no day go by in which I do not bless Thee," (his commentary on psalm 144). Thomas Merton, reflecting on Augustine's words, clinched it by noting that words of praise "establish us in God."[14]

I have days in which I am extremely un-"established" in God. I awake in fear. I feel depressed. I forget my purpose. I want to forget! The day ahead seems too tedious to face. And you? On such mornings it is so useful to remember this injunction to praise. To praise the raw miracle of life, to merely breathe and know myself to be alive and thus still in the realm of possibility for anything, doesn't make the other stuff go away, but clearly re-orients my head. Praise ennobles me; such praise is the work of a human being whose true nature is one of intrinsic dignity.

As Thomas Merton noted about the psalms, they are "songs without plan, because there are no blueprints for ecstasy." Our poems of praise are building our faith. The same may be said for those who read them, sing them, pray them. Although words will never fully reflect the greatness of Love, prayers of praise do help to elaborate for us *who* this Love is.

Rabbi Abraham Heschel advised his congregation that "praise precedes faith." He urged them to immerse themselves in their liturgy, which was based in praise. We can do the same. Those of us who care to immerse ourselves in a practice of praise, using our own or others' litanies of worship, will soak up its mood and begin to realize what it reflects. In doing so we will find an immeasurable treasure. Whether we know anything of theology, we will somehow absorb an organic gratitude, based in our awe at the greatness of existence. Praying the psalms or other forms, we praise. Singing the name of God, calling upon the Divine in every circumstance of our lives, we are slowly opened, the way a bud unfolds imperceptibly in the light of the sun. Our fragile and tiny seed of faith begins to stir. Sending out roots, it grows. And miraculously, joyfully, we are renewed.

> "If you have faith of the size of this mustard seed you will say to this mountain 'Move,' and the mountain will move."                                     —Matthew 17, 20-21.

Clearly, we are in desperate need of such mountain-moving faith in our times. The psalms, prayer and poetry of gratitude and exultation is a way to that faith.

# 8. Chanting the Name of God

In a recent time of internal chaos—this one characterized by self-loathing, fear, a sense of overwhelm and great loneliness, all rolled up into one dark interior cloud—I found myself turning to the name of God as a source of stability. I really wasn't begging God for relief from all of it. The chaos was *what was*, and despite the fact that it felt like hell, there wasn't any real compulsion to drive it away. I knew, somehow, that I was caught deeply in some vortex of the illusion, flailing around, being thrown from internal pillar to internal post in the dialogues that went on in my mind and on the roller coaster of emotions that these dialogues were generating. Somehow I knew that none of these feelings and sensations was true in any objective sense. What I looked for was not another illusion of imaginary relief but something real. The name of God was that.

Another way to describe my experience—I was lost at sea and all of a sudden a sturdy lifeboat was given to me. I clung to that lifeboat. A lifeboat doesn't abate a storm. The storm still rages. The lifeboat only gives one a point of reference for stability. The name of God was my lifeboat. Repeating the name of God, a sweetness grew within. Clarity of vision emerged. Strength to go on was found, despite the storm.

We in the Western world don't really have much foundation for the power of a word, a name. In the Hindu tradition they speak of chanting as a means of changing the vibration of the life around and in us, as well as releasing the deity trapped or hidden within the words. Either of these approaches is a radical departure from our training in general semantics in which we learned, as the number one rule, that the map was not the territory. So, this business of saying the name of God is decidedly a new domain for most of us.

Several fantastic stories, each of which I heard firsthand, touch upon the reality of this hidden power of the word. An old acquaintance of mine is a shaman who has worked for many years in South America. He told me that he and the other shamans in his region commonly accepted that, when confronted with forces or entities that were unknown and threatening, especially when under threat of death, that intentionally invoking the name "Jesus Christ" was the most powerful tool against such forces, the most effective form of protection.

I know of two cases, one of a man and one of a woman, both friends of mine, who were being attacked—the woman was threatened with rape, the man with robbery. In each case the person under attack spontaneously used the name of God as their shield; neither of them would have planned such a response. The woman turned to her attacker and said with power and confidence, "In the name of God I command you to release me." The attacker fled. In the man's case, he shouted the name of his teacher's master, "Yogi Ramsuratkumar" with full voice. His attacker fled.

An ancient Tibetan religious practice involved the placing of *termas*. The word *terma* means "hidden treasure," and refers to relics and texts that were purportedly hidden by the great master Padmasambhava and his disciples in Tibet during the eighth century as a means of protecting and preserving these teachings. To say they were hidden is actually an understatement. *Termas* were not just placed in the far reaches of caves but sometimes embedded in solid rock, or grown into the bark of trees. How the *terma* gets placed into solid rock or into the bark of a tree is part of the shamanistic magic of that culture. Centuries later, such *termas* can be located by those specially trained in such arts. The *terton*, or one who discovers the treasure, is a practitioner of the highest yogic powers—through their power of attention and careful listening they are able to unlock what others overlook. The idea is that the *termas* are revealed when the world is in need of their particular message.

The idea of a *terma* runs a strong parallel to the power of the word locked into the *mantra* or the name of God. Like a tiny tabernacle, the word contains the deity, but the deity will not be released without attentive focus, sometimes the focus of years.

Another way in which our Western education is lacking is in the science of vibration. Despite the fact that we have seen (at least on film) that glass will shatter with certain high pitched frequencies, or that certain kinds of music will literally cause a vibration in the body (I feel this particularly when listening to violins), we are naïve in this domain. We may scoff at the notion that tuning forks placed on the body could actually bring about pain relief, even though there are accepted allopathic medical practices of implanting electrical neurotransmitters in the spine to block pain signals to the brain. Are we to believe that a particular sound could actually affect a change in the internal chemistry of the body? Yet, that is what the repetition of the name of God can be. The Sufis have ninety-nine names of Allah, each supposedly with a unique vibrational quality, and each with unique features for effecting an alchemical change in the body of the practitioner who chants this sacred name.

When I visited my teacher's guru in India in 1995 I was captured by the chanting of his name. It permeated every aspect of life in the Indian ashram, where hundreds of devotees sang it day and night. And, when I returned to the states, my sleep was still interrupted by this constant drone. I remember a moment, sitting at my desk on a Friday afternoon, when I realized that I had a choice of what to think about in a particular moment. Apparently, the thought process slowed down enough to allow for that tiny intervention of awareness. The choice was to think about some situation that was currently brewing in my personal life or to chant the name of God and simply allow that name to take full possession of my mind. I recall feeling a momentary panic—what if my thinking ended all together and nothing went on in this brain except for this chant? Could that be insanity? How would I accomplish my business? What would I ever have to say to my husband?

Yet, in that moment, the pull of the Divine power trapped within the name was so compelling that I went with it, allowing the future to take care of itself, which it obviously did.

I did not go insane (at least I don't think I did). Nor did that degree of heightened awareness stay with me beyond the space of a few weeks. Like all experiences, it faded. With this moment, however, I experienced directly what it would be like to surrender the mind. What did happen was actually quite astounding. Another mind—a larger mind, you might say—took over and seemed to direct the show. The mind that was anchored in the past was no longer the predominant mind. The constant inner dialogue that usually tired me out was no longer running things. That internal dialogue was not gone completely, it just went on in a room at the back of the house in my mind.

Since that point, and again most recently since writing this book, the name of God has continued to grow more and more attractive for me. Lately I surmise that saying the name of God is about simply declaring things in their rightful place—God first, all else second. When God is praised and acknowledged under all circumstance, all things are made obvious and clear. This is exactly the message contained in the popular spiritual classic *The Way of the Pilgrim*, the story of a nineteenth-century Russian man who used the name of God in the Jesus Prayer as the means of praying unceasingly.

I think there is a mystery under our noses that we are not taking advantage of because we are so steeped in a certain logical orientation. Our brain structures will hardly allow us to violate their patterning for meaning. Can we at least entertain the possibility that there is more going on about the conscious use of the name of God than we know? I suggest that *mantra*, especially as it involves *japa*, or repetition of the name of God, is something that could be of extreme benefit to us. I would highly recommend an exploration into the power of such words, these holy names, to learn for ourselves what is hidden there.

Our habits of prayer are a means of carrying us through life on purpose, rather than simply being blown around. Part of our work in the domain of prayer is to build what in Gurdjieffian terminology are called "essence habits."[15] These are the habits that will naturally kick in when we are out of our mind—whether because we find ourselves in some "corridor of madness" as E. J. Gold has described,[16] or some variation of the "dark night of the soul," as St. John of the Cross has described,[17] or some situation of extreme boredom or even deprivation, some externally tragic or threatening situation. Our habit of chanting the name of God could become such an essence habit. Our habit of laying down all our concerns at the feet of God could become an essence habit. Our habit of visualization of the Lord residing in the temple of the heart could become an essence habit. Our habit of breathing to return to the center of ourselves could become an essence habit leading to focus, concentration and balance. Any and all of these internal habits could serve us well when the going gets rough.

Invoking the name of God allows us to return to the context of prayer, to the context of the present moment, to the context of "big mind," which is the context of all things in and as the Divine. These are priceless gifts. Using the name of God can draw us back to reality, momentarily waking us from the world of illusion, wherein we frolic and fret in innumerable dreams and projections.

## 9. The Prayer of Remembered Purpose

As we set out down the driveway, a full fifteen-passenger van enroute to the airport where we would take off on a European tour, my teacher passed around a few photocopied sheets of paper on which was printed a travel prayer. It was an auspicious morning. Over the years that I have been in my teacher's company he has only given us three other formal prayers to be used on specific occasions—a meal prayer, a birth prayer and a death prayer. As the community spread to Europe, and as trips to India became a yearly occurrence, the travel prayer was a welcome addition.

A line in this travel prayer reads: "May we never forget our purpose." A phrase like that is embarrassing to say, simply because over and over it makes me aware of just how lacking in remembered purpose I have been and am in the moment of saying it. "My purpose?" Oh, yeah.

A few years ago I spent two days with a woman, Jean, whose example of diligent purpose was sterling. We were assigned a mission together—she was coming to the Scottsdale area to visit a mutual friend who was ill, and had asked me to accompany her. I jumped at the chance.

Jean had the kind of invisible discipline that permeated everything she did. To say she was a warrior would be to assign something grand to something which was so ordinary, but that is exactly the way her behavior struck me. She was a woman with a purpose, and nothing was going to distract her from that.

The incidents I remember most clearly were our trips to the supermarket to shop for dinner and to the drug store to buy her a new pair of sunglasses, as her eyes were assaulted by the Arizona daylight. She walked into the drugstore and went straight to the sunglasses rack, took off one pair, tried them on, and turned and walked directly to the check-out counter. I was still adjusting the mirror at the top of the rack, wondering whether I could justify buying myself another pair of sunglasses, even though I already had two.

Her intention and her lack of distraction was the same in the supermarket. She chose the vegetables with precision— her eagle eye scanning the arrangement of tomatoes, without touching and squeezing them, and then landing on the one she would take (which turned out to be perfectly ripe). I knew I was in the presence of an artist, one whose economy of energy usage was refined to the point of mastery. She had no intention of wasting the energy that could be used in the sanctuary of prayer in the vortexes of distractions offered by the supermarket.

How many times over the years had I found myself wandering the aisles of supermarkets asking myself what I was really looking for. I was looking for a way to distract myself from the intensity of a life of annihilation, or from the burn of facing my ego's illusions, by putting my attention on the racks of hair ornaments, or the varieties of bottled water. It didn't matter what distracted me, it was all the same. It was all wasting, wasting, wasting the energy of prayer in the realm of illusion.

So, "may we never forget our purpose" is a dangerous prayer because it cuts off miles of aisles of potential distraction.

What a way to live!

As a young nun I was impressed with a story of Bernard of Clairvaux, the saintly monk of the Middle Ages who founded the Cistercian Order, commonly known as the Trappists. Bernard, it seems, would begin every day with the same prayer—actually a form of self-inquiry and remembrance that was recommended by other monastics. "Bernard, Bernard," he would ask himself, "why have you come here?"

One can imagine Bernard rising from a bed of straw, struck with the cold of his solitary cell in the dead of winter in the early hours of the morning, the bell that summons the monks to Matins, the first hour of the Divine Office, still echoing through the lonely corridors. Groggy from sleep, he throws off a thin cover and stands, orienting to the waking world from his comforting dreams. And then the force of resistance strikes—as it strikes every monk, every mother, every athlete, every one of us. "What am I doing this for?" we ask ourselves. Am I crazy? Why bother? The variations of doubt and resistance are endless and some are more compelling and seductive than others. Every cell in the body begs to crawl back into the safe womb, even if it is only a pile of straw. The allure of sleep —sleep for the body, or sleep for the consciousness burdened by responsibility for the world—is great.

Why *do* we get up?

Bernard's habitual question intervenes now, disturbing the downward spiral that would draw him into unconsciousness. His question: "Why have you come here?" is answered in his unique way, which was not part of the story as I heard it. We can only guess. But answered it was, and in a way that set his day on course, like the programming of a computer that will guide a spacecraft. Once set, the astronaut need only put his or her body in its appropriate seat and make the necessary adjustments all along the way.

"What gets you out of bed in the morning?" the workshop leader asked in a seminar I attended. Along with the other participants, I struggled to peel away the layers of superficiality that characterized my initial discomfort with the question.

"The alarm clock," many of us joked.

"But why set the alarm clock?" he asked.

"Because I have to get to work on time ..."

"But, why are you working ..." the leader persisted.

And on and on he went with further questioning, not letting us be satisfied even when we thought we'd reached the bottom line. Our difficulty with the question urged us to realize how mechanical we were and how lacking in self-directed or at least consciously-invoked purpose our lives were.

Without a purpose we are lost. Without a purpose bigger than our own comfort and self-preservation, we are destined to mediocrity. Even if we think we have a purpose, or had a purpose, we are doomed to wander the labyrinth again and again hitting the center only randomly if we neglect to remember that purpose. Our prayer, however, can be our means to remember and to reaffirm what we have come for ... or why we are getting up in the morning. A prayer of remembered purpose will disrupt and redirect a life. We can use whatever words we want, but whatever purpose we take (and we are free to take any number of them) is going to take on a life of its own. Our purpose, if renewed consistently, is going to swallow us up, whether it is a worthy purpose or not.

In an interview for the magazine *What is Enlightenment*, Ma Jaya Sati Bhagavati, who has dedicated her life to serving the dying, particularly those dying from AIDS, straightforwardly revealed her practice of remembering purpose. Speaking to Andrew Cohen, her interviewer, about her concern for the suffering of humanity and the terrible state of the environment, she remarked, "As soon as I'm finished speaking to you, I'm going to retake my vows to serve even more. Because what I speak, I must do."[18]

# 10. "O God Be Merciful to Me, A Sinner"

The notion of sin is so out of vogue today. Perhaps for good reason. Awful tyranny has been wrought on the human spirit by those who have preached a gospel of sin as a means of keeping the masses in line. What greater form of tyranny than to pervert the conscience of the man or woman who truly wants to love and serve, rendering genuine conscience as nothing more than an internalized punishing parent who never allows for pleasure or spontaneity. Good riddance to that one!

Yet the paradox remains that some of the greatest spiritual masters have spoken seriously of sin, some even include the recognition of sin as central to the mystical ascent. Those who wish to climb this holy mountain of God, armed with the prayer that will be their very oxygen, are well advised to rethink, or re-feel, this relationship to sin, and not to throw it out too easily, rejecting the truth it may contain.

My teacher's guru, who died in February 2001 at eighty-two, was a beggar who lived in southern India. When I had the chance to visit Yogi Ramsuratkumar for five weeks in 1995, I left convinced of his constant prayer and communion with the Divine, whom he affectionately called his "Father," as did the great master Jesus before him. Without knowing the technology or the cosmology of his work, I somehow knew that his prayer was a force for universal good. I could sense that his preoccupation ("All is Father, everything is Father ..." was a phrase he used all the time) was perhaps one means of effectively keeping our sick and sorry world from falling off the brink on which it precariously balanced.

The old beggar was a living conundrum to the rational mind—dressed in rags, he moved with the grace of a king. His way was completely irrelevant in terms of worldly accomplishment, yet anyone who took the time to simply sit in his presence, allowing the mind to be subsumed by the energy that surrounded him, could not help but come away with the sense that something of enormous value existed there, whether one could speak what that was or not.

The old beggar rarely used the personal pronoun. Instead, he spoke some derogatory title like "madman" or "beggar" when referring to himself. But a term he most used was one that caused his devotees the most consternation: "this dirty sinner."

In the West, as we speak and write of Yogi Ramsuratkumar, confounded by his continual reference to being a sinner, we often struggle to make it something wondrous. "Oh, how humble this great one is," we say with devotion dripping from our tongues. We are loathe to face the possibility that this same one to whom we are so devoted, this one who embodies love for us, is in fact telling us a truth that we must take to heart. By his own admission, his sin was always before him, as close as his name. There is a connection, I believe, between his recognition of his sin and his exalted holiness. A connection that all of us can profit from learning.

We are all sinners before the Absolute. Regardless of our inherent perfection in our imperfection, we all find ourselves consciously or unconsciously contributing to racism and war and poverty and meanness of spirit; we all find self-satisfaction paramount to the care of others—not just once or twice, but over and over again, everyday. What else is this but sin, not necessarily even my sin or your sin, but sin nonetheless? Our world and we in it may be helpless to be otherwise, but the fact remains that without reference to the source of love itself, we are a sad and sorry race of solipsists. We are only redeemed, truly forgiven, saved from a life of loathing and self-absorption, by acknowledgement of the "basic goodness" of the essence ... or the love of God.

Such recognition of our helplessness, our meanness, our refusal and our fear opens us to the reality of the human condition that must be faced as a stage in any process of purification. We cannot be purified from a distance. We can't take out our minds or our souls and throw them into a vat of Clorox, while we sit in the waiting room reading a magazine. The purification of our pettiness, which is all motivated by our firm belief in our separation from the One, must be grappled with, and endured with every cell in the body.

There is great value in speaking of sin and telling the truth about our participation in it. Prayer will bring sin roaring into our faces. Such sin will rise up before us like a hideous monster. We will be sickened by the recognition of its insidious penetration into every action that we perform; sickened to see that *everything* is self-referenced rather than love-referenced. We will be depressed to the point of despair by the helplessness we feel in the midst of trying to make a difference. And, right smack dab in the center of our terrible dread, our full confession of our sin, we have the greatest possibility to give up the fight and lay ourselves and all our weapons down.

I recommend that we just sit with the pain of our sin. I suggest that we take courage, refuse to enter again into denial, and let ourselves drown and be drowned in our pain and remorse. Be helpless and hopeless. We won't know how much we need to be found if we keep denying that we are lost. We've got to lose. We've got to drown in the misery of the situation, our own situation, and the situation of poor humanity, if we ever want to know genuine compassion as opposed to some warm cuddly sense of okay-ness. Only when we begin from the premise of our sleeping state do we have any chance to experience awakening.

Drowning, we will sink into a great paradox. At first it will seem as if we have reached the end of it all. And well it should. But, if we are really drowning, if we are really going under, we will cry out. We will struggle for all that we are worth. We will pray at last from the cells of our whole body, "O God, be merciful to me, a poor sinner." This prayer, traditionally in the Orthodox Christian traditions called the Prayer of the Heart, the Jesus Prayer, or something akin to it in whatever language we pray, is a cry that elicits genuine transformation. Only in acknowledging our utter helplessness can we be undone without our own interference. Half measures only allow us to intervene too quickly. Genuine desperation draws the Divine like nothing else.

Our cry for help may not be said in exactly those words. But the sentiments, the intention, these will be what makes it all happen. Here, at the bottom of the world, at the bottom of the deepest well, at the bottom of my life, feeling at the edge of desolation, alone, without help, I admit that I have chosen sin when love was offered, and selfishness was my response. And now that I see that, I can see that throughout my life I have been clinging to my sin as a means of self-definition, or as a means of avoiding a deeper pain, and now I realize that I can give it all away. I have no more need to hold onto it as my security.

Isn't that the strangest thing, that we both deny our sin and yet cling to our sin—both strategies of separation? I think we never go quite far enough into our sin—The sin, The pain—to be transformed by it, and we never allow ourselves to let it go enough that it can be transformed into something else.

My teacher has told me that God wants our sins. Our pride, our vanity, our greed, our anger, he says, are gifts of interest and attractiveness to the Divine. Such substance is usable to God. Life is healed when these foods are left at the altar of sacrifice.

And when we see our sin, what then? I think we should avoid asking God for forgiveness, but rather ask God for open eyes. Ask God for a way to see what is really going on. Ask for clarity. Ask for a knowledge of the underworld that we have been denying.

Let us be courageous. Let us not flinch. Let us go the whole distance. Let us pray to finally pray: "O God, mercy, mercy. Come."

All hail the awesome possibility of prayer!

## A Dangerous Prayer in the Face of My Sin

I who wish to pray, am I really willing to be broken again? Am I willing to be faced again with all the denial of my life? Am I willing to mourn a broken life, and broken dreams, and missed opportunities, and words of cruelty, and doors closed in the face of friends, and plotted revenge and indifference, and worst of all, perhaps, of designing a safe haven so that I wouldn't have to suffer like the rest, which is my sin, the sin of the spiritually elite?

Am I willing to look at the selfishness that drove me to not have children, and the selfishness that drives others to have children, and the unimaginable ways in which we have all disappointed children, and crushed their dreams, and made them afraid? Am I willing to look at my enormous insensitivity in demanding children's conformity, my own conformity, the conformity of others? Am I willing to look at my advanced practice of ass-kissing for the sake of protection and for the sake of getting ahead? O God, these are my sins. I am overwhelmed. And there are more.

Am I willing to feel the horror of my lies? O, how I have lied to protect myself and to win! I have failed to honor my word. I have been a great hypocrite. I have flaunted my ideas and ideals about love, but I have not let myself be broken by love. I have hidden myself from what would be dangerous to my heart. And, saddest of all, I have kept myself in denial that I was doing all of this. O Love, these are my sins, and there are more.

Dear God, today I drown in the knowledge of the failure of poor humans. And, it is good, I think, to recognize myself as a guilty bystander in all of this. Today I feel the pain of poor humanity, and myself not separate from that; humanity unconscious of itself, choosing safety, choosing pleasure in the short run, choosing fear because it is familiar, choosing power because it seems like security ... security against death. O God, how pathetic I am; how pathetic we are, poor creatures. Let me feel the awful horror of human horror. O God, the situation is horrible when I forget my soul and pick up weapons that will only destroy myself. O God, this dread is deep. And God, I thank you for letting me feel it. Amen.

—RSR

## 11. "To Die Before I Die"

We might imagine that if we had a reminding factor, something to keep us remembering our purpose all throughout the day, we would have little trouble in realizing the fruits of a life of prayer. And yet we do have this reminding factor, we simply don't believe it. We are all going to die. Period.

A famous Christian treatise on prayer recommends that beginners (and aren't we all) bring an urgency to their prayer by simply imagining that in fact this period of prayer might be the very last opportunity they have in which to open themselves to communion with God. Truth is, we don't have any guarantee that this moment won't be our last; that this meditation might not be the one that carries us into eternity, or into our next life.

A Buddhist prayer reflects the same truth—the absolute impermanence of all things:

If I carefully examine all the beings, distinguished and lowly, who lived in the past, I find that now only their names remain. And of all the beings who are living now, every one of them will someday pass away.

Since my present status, house, relatives, friends, possessions, and even this body must all pass away without remaining for long, to what am I attached in this dream-like present?

A good life that is truly meaningful is always difficult to find, and when found is impermanent and will quickly be destroyed like a dewdrop that clings to a blade of grass.

—from *Essence of Nectar*,
prayers of Lama Tsongkhopa[19]

And from Sufism we have the preeminent teaching, "Die before you die," a statement attributed to the Prophet Muhammad. This phrase describes the voluntary death to self that characterizes the spiritual path:

> This death or extinction has ten conditions: repentance, asceticism, trust, contentment, detachment, attention to invocation, perfect attentiveness towards God, patience, contemplation and satisfaction. These conditions are in fact the stages of the Sufi path and have been described differently by differently Masters … The one constant is the need for a guide.[20]

In light of these considerations it might prove helpful to create a formal death prayer for ourselves, using words that carry some potency, in which we acknowledge the impermanence of our lives, the realization that nothing guarantees the next breath, and our desire to die to self. This would be exactly the prayer to use dozens of times a day, with the thousands of tiny challenges that are offered us, especially challenges of discomfort. Every time we are presented with the invaluable opportunity to undermine self-importance, to take a back seat so that others can be served first, to keep our mouth shut when what we have to say is irrelevant or unkind, we die a little. A good death. Every time we must bear the thoughtlessness of others, or endure their annoying habits, we can die a little more, if we bear and endure consciously, without collecting points for being so long-suffering. Every time we make a mistake, miss the mark, or put our foot in our mouth, consciously lose face or fall on our face, we die to who we think we are in order that who we truly are may be born.

To consciously practice dying in living becomes a joy. Prayer transforms unconscious gestures and reactions into useable energy-food. Praying in this way we learn that it is more blessed and much more fun to always be new, to be slightly off balance, to be available to others rather than to live for our own comfort and convenience. We build our inner life with such transformations. The purpose of a death prayer—in this case a prayer of dedication of our little sacrifices—would be to sharpen our focus, to help to diminish the extreme diffuseness of our minds, which simply reflects the diffuse focus of our life in general.

I practice dying when I am a passenger in an airplane. (See Chapter 10 for more about prayer in transit.) I've always been a nervous flyer. At the root of it all, I don't want to die, and I especially don't want to die in an inferno, or by free-falling from 30,000 feet (to name a few of my favorite and most horrific fantasies). Over many years I've observed my unconscious airline prayers—all superstitious petitions, coupled with positive visualizations, and all aimed at making me feel better about being out of control, left in the hands of the pilot and his computer, which is what airline flight means to me.

Flying in an airplane is a great place to practice dying, to observe something about the nature of surrender, and even to take the reins by creating a prayer of complete abandonment to the will of God. Imagine having the courage to pray, as many have before us, "I accept and embrace whatever form my death will take." Imagine applying that prayer every day of your life, in all circumstances, like when a sharp pain awakens you in the night. Instead of panic followed by a prayer for relief, what about the use of a prayer of letting go into God, *first*; and only then, when the context of our orientation to death has been established, or at least intended, seeking tangible help or relief as necessary.

Imagine a further dedication still, whereby our death was offered as a living prayer, a means of praising God, an alignment with the organic cycles of creation, sustenance and destruction rather than with the view of death as failure and tragedy. Any prayer that orients us in this shift of context is a dangerous prayer indeed.

Ultimately, as the mystics and saints have instructed us, we should be praying always, which means throughout life and right through death. Imagine being so present to life that one is fully aware as the physical body dies as well. The mystics and masters have also informed us that what we call death is but an illusion. If indeed we are the Pure Consciousness … if indeed we are not and never will be separate from God … if we are the Perfect that has unfolded from the Perfect … then death as we commonly think of it is a lie. What if our prayer reflected that? What if we simply held to this reality by choice—a choice to trust—even when we had no immediate feeling sense of this reality. Over time, our intentions would catalyze into knowing.

The interplay of all these realizations are nowhere more apparent than in the so-called "death poems" of numerous Buddhist Zen teachers and Japanese haiku poets. Traditionally, such masters would compose a last poem as they approached the occasion of physical death; a poem that summed up their teaching or level of insight; as well as a poem that reflected their relationship to death.

Suzuki Shosan was both a teacher and a samurai. Throughout his teaching work he proposed that one "… look straight at death. To know death—that is the entire doctrine."[21] Shosan became ill in the spring of 1655, at the age of seventy-seven. When he was informed of the severity of his illness, "he said that it meant nothing, since he had already died more than thirty years before." It was thirty years earlier that he had become a monk. "As his condition became critical his followers gathered around his deathbed. One of them asked him to say 'final words.' Shosan looked sharply at the monk and scolded him: 'What are you saying? You only show that you don't understand what I've been saying for more than thirty years. Like this, I simply die.'"[22]

And Musho Josho, who died in 1306, wrote:

When it comes—just so!
When it goes—just so!
Both coming and going occur each day.
The words I am speaking now—just so?[23]

The fear of death keeps us in prison. But, as we practice and learn to die to self-interest, then discomfort and inconvenience and the opinions of others will have less power over us, and we will be free to serve, regardless. Such flagrant disregard of the grasping usually associated with life is the basis for spiritual life, and the basis of true prayer.

Isn't it time to put first things first, as we've always wanted them? Isn't it time to put God's will above everything else? Awareness of our death and the nature of impermanence can help us in living out what we say we want.

# IX

# PEOPLE OF
# DANGEROUS PRAYER

We learn to pray in many different ways. Primarily, when we make the intention to pray, asking for the help of the Spirit, we are instructed through the internal revelation that comes to us through the body—some call this the heart, or the gut, or the holy spirit, or the wisdom of the cells. But, we also receive seeds of the teaching about prayer from the religious traditions in which we were raised, from books we read, and in the services or rituals of genuine devotion that we are fortunate to attend. Some of these seeds remain dormant for years until conditions are right for their germination. Sometimes it is through personal devastation or sorrow that the soil of the soul becomes moist enough to encourage the seed to life.

Perhaps the most precious of these seeds is that given to us by contact with a person who embodies the essence of prayer. Even if they have been dead for centuries, contact with great men and women of prayer is still possible as we read of them or hear their stories. Their relationship to the Divine, their passion for the truth, their very prayers, as well as their example, lives on, and we catch these seeds of inspiration and guidance. Beyond that and a rarer gift still, to actually see prayer in person by contact with a living human being who makes prayer tangible and even irresistible to us.

The essays that follow contain many precious seeds. Each of the people mentioned in this section has given me something about the nature of prayer, particularly about dangerous or transformational prayer, through their words or through their lives. They are certainly not an exclusive nor an exhaustive group; many of the teachings about prayer that I have received are not listed here, and each reader would undoubtedly have his or her own collection to celebrate and remember. The ones that are included, however, are those that seemingly took on a life of their own and demanded a place in this book—for one or more reasons. I simply couldn't refuse. May they inspire you to prayer as they have inspired me.

# 1. URSULA AT PRAYER

I remember the doorkeeper.

Sister Ursula was probably in her late forties when I first knew her. I was eighteen and newly arrived at the huge, rambling old building on Blue Point Ave. that served as the motherhouse for the Ursuline nuns. This was the place where we postulants (first year aspirants) and novices (second and third year nuns-in-training) lived and studied in our preparation for vows.

The doorkeeper's job was awesome in this house. No matter where Sister Ursula was, day or night, or what she was involved in at the time, her duty was to stop and then run to answer the bell.

The entry to the front door of the convent was reached only by a long, highly polished corridor, leading into the carpeted parlors that sprawled into small sitting rooms. At the end of this labyrinth was the entry door.

I can see Sister Ursula wiping her hands on her well-worn apron, untying it as she ran, unsnapping the tabs that had allowed her to hike up her long black dress, which we all did to keep our dresses clean and to be able to work less encumbered. I remember her breathlessly making her way to that door, then composing herself as she tucked a few stray hairs into her headdress, fixing a broad smile on her face and opening the door.

Ursula was a large, robust woman. Not heavy, just big-boned, with the kind of hands that are too big for women's-sized gloves, and the kind of feet that are always squeezed into a shoe that is too narrow. Ursula belonged on the farm, tending the farm animals. But we didn't have a farm. We were a teaching order of nuns, but that is neither here nor there.

She had a reputation, Ursula did. And as naïve as we were, postulants and novices, we didn't question what was so obvious. Ursula's reputation was for holiness—we didn't have many more words for her than that. I had watched Ursula pray. I'd steal glances at her across the chapel aisle, where she sat in the last bench, ready to run. With her eyes closed she didn't know she was being watched. But watch her I did, and her body spoke to me, to us, about this potency, this prayer that we were mere apprentices to.

What was she doing in *there?* In that lovely interior of herself?

I could only guess that whatever she *did* must be much more profound than the frittery stuff dancing in my head. Whatever it was, it had a depth that beckoned and drew me in—the way one feels when standing back from the edge of a cliff: fascinated, compelled to look, yet terrified. Without ever putting words to it I just knew that Ursula loved God, and I *knew* that God loved Ursula. The homely, oversized features of her face, her worn hands and her sturdy body were radiantly beautiful in prayer. I knew then what it meant that one could be the bride, the spouse, of Jesus. After all, weren't all brides beautiful?

At the time, it never struck me as the least bit strange that Ursula could be praying intently, seemingly lost in some otherworldly realm, and still leap to her feet at the sound of a bell, and run. Yet today, as I think of Sister Ursula and what her body—whether at rest or in motion—taught us about prayer, I am grateful that this communication was made to me so tangibly at such an early stage in my life. Ursula taught us our primary lessons in praying dangerously. She instructed us that there was no gap, no dichotomy between spiritual exercises and daily responsibilities; no problem with integrating a life of devotion with a life of action. Not only was she always ready to be interrupted from spiritual pursuits—it was, in fact, her job to be interrupted! We knew that she had the Lord in her heart—it was so obvious. I'll bet she knew she would find Him at the front door as well.

## 2. RABI-A AT PRAYER

O my Lord, if I worship Thee from fear of Hell,
burn me in Hell,
And if I worship Thee from hope of Paradise,
exclude me from thence,
But if I worship Thee for Thine own sake then
withhold not from me
Thine Eternal Beauty.

—Rabi'a of Basra (8th century)[1]

Rabi'a was a dangerous woman, and a great Sufi mystic of the eighth century. She was dangerous in the way that all single-minded people are dangerous. She challenged polite conventionality; she would not bend to a lesser way. She lived by the radically uncompromising principles expressed in this prayer.

How she learned to pray, which is the same question as how she earned the passionate dedication that characterized her life, history does not reveal. Because she was orphaned as a child and soon after sold into slavery, it was undoubtedly a path of suffering that wore away her defenses, causing her to rely solely on the One, the Lord, whom she affectionately referred to as "the Beloved."

Legend recounts that Rabi'a was freed from slavery by her master after he witnessed a most remarkable event. One night he was awakened from sleep by a light streaming into his room. Rising from bed and walking to the window, he surveyed the courtyard below, the location from which the light was emanating. There, kneeling in prayer, was the young slave girl, Rabi'a. Above her head, suspended in mid-air, was an oil lamp with a flame so bright that it illuminated the whole area like a newly risen full moon. What was the man to do? He wisely let her go.

From the day of her release until the day of her death, Rabi'a relied solely upon the benediction of God—fasting when there was no food, sleeping under a tree when there was no shelter, interpreting every circumstance of her life as a direct expression of her Beloved's good pleasure for her. "God alone" was Rabia's dangerous prayer and her dangerous life.

One story about her concerns a beautiful home that she was given by a devoted follower. Ordinarily she spent most of her time wandering, teaching by the example of her life and enormous passion for the Beloved. When not in transit she lived in a shack, which she termed a "ruin"—an apt description not only for her dwelling place but for her life in the opinion of the world. On the momentous day in which she first set foot in the new home and looked around, she turned her back on it, never to return. Aghast, her devotees inquired of her leaving. Rabi'a explained, in no uncertain terms, that she was afraid that she might fall in love with a house, thereby risking distraction for a moment from her Beloved's gaze.

Her prayer for the worship of God for God's own sake is echoed in the writing of an unknown cleric of the fourteenth century, the author of the famous Christian classic on prayer, *The Cloud of Unknowing*:

> Love is pure when you ask God neither for release from suffering, nor for increase of joy, nor for the sweetness of his love here below—except when you need sweetness to freshen up your spiritual forces lest you should fail—but when you ask from God only himself. Then you neither care nor consider whether you are in pain or bliss, so long as you love him whom you love.[2]

What an amazing standard! Can we in the twenty-first century possibly aspire to such totally pure motivation, as distracted as our lives are by factors that seem beyond our control in this culture? Yet, if we didn't pray until our intention was this clear, completely free of our fear and our grasping, could we ever pray at all?

The prayers of Rabi'a and other mystics should not be used against ourselves—we would be fools to berate ourselves for our lack of one-pointedness, greater fools to dismiss such prayer as totally unattainable. Such standards as these prayers represent can draw us up, can inspire us. Maybe we can even use Rabi'a as a guide in prayer, asking for her direction, asking her to reveal her secret to us—I have no doubt that Rabi'a was not so different from me as I might initially suspect. Whether her biographers will ever discover how and why, I know that like me, at one time or another, she had to suffer through stages of resistance and immaturity in order to grow up spiritually. I know that what we read about in her prayers, and in those of the author of the *Cloud*, is the result of a lifetime (or more) of refinement. The mature, ripe spirituality that such prayers reveal is hard earned, at the very least in the patience it takes to endure the years of its ripening. Praying dangerously is a lifetime proposition, for certainly it may take a lifetime, or maybe more than one, to pray a pure prayer, or for our prayer to ever reach such a lofty clarity as Rabi'a's prayer did.

Rabi'a teaches us about a mature relationship to God and a mature relationship to the present moment—two important lessons for our times. Anticipation of the rewards of heaven and the fears of punishment in hell translate to being lost in the past or distracted by the future. Whether we are begging God for some future goals, even a worthy goal like enlightenment, or worrying about past sins, or extolling past virtues that we hope are accumulating interest in some spiritual bank account, we are missing the mark. Both types of preoccupation cause us to leave the raw *suchness* of the present moment, the only place where God is found. Only here and only now is there a possibility to love God. All the rest is fantasy.

The worship of God for God's own sake is simply another way of saying that I get left behind while God alone remains. Such a self-forgetting that places the All, the One, the power of love, at the center of the mandala of life, is what Rabi'a models for us in her prayer. I think this is not so far from our intention in taking up contemplative or transformational prayer in the first place. Like Rabi'a, we intuit that this is our rightful place in creation—lost to ego, alive to love.

I think that by far the hardest part of this teaching about prayer is the invitation to drop the punisher/rewarder dichotomy in relation to God. Easy to say, not so easy to do. Such images and understandings of the Divine as mean judge and jury or as benevolent Santa Claus are deeply soaked in our cells, from our own experience and from the experience of many generations before us. Very early on, based in our need to survive, we saw Mommy or Daddy as God, and we learned to be wary of that God. Mommies and daddies were unpredictable. They did reward and punish us, all the time—sometimes for reasons that we couldn't fathom. Now, despite the fact that we are grownups, in some ways we are still like timid children in our approach to God. Having been threatened with punishment, abandonment or disapproval so many times, we are loathe to trust anyone we perceive to be in that powerful a position. Nonetheless, we create God in this image and then rebel against this God, and rightly so.

While our rational adult mind knows otherwise, it takes time for the love and constancy of the true God to reveal itself, so thick are our attachments to false gods. Rabi'a's teaching is a call to tear down our fortress walls. She is urging us to really grow up; to expose ourselves to the healing force of love in prayer; to face God for God's own sake. As we risk falling into the emptiness of a God other than one who rewards and punishes, we are oriented toward a radical stand, a radical way of life—beyond good and bad, beyond sin and virtue, even beyond bliss or fear. Such standing on nothing ... NOTHING ... causes an internal transformation. Heat is generated when we refuse to fall back upon old habits of either groveling or defending ourselves in relationship to God; things get hotter when we don't condemn ourselves for our sins or count up our spiritual goody-points. With such heat we are slowly baked into wholeness, like a good custard that starts out soupy and ends up firm. That wholeness is a relationship with a God of love.

# 3. LEE LOZOWICK'S BAD PRAYERS

"I don't know anything about prayer."
—Lee Lozowick

On a tiny ashram in the desert of northern Arizona lived a man of dangerous prayer. For over twenty-five years, Lee Lozowick, my spiritual teacher, wrote poem-prayers to his own spiritual master, Yogi Ramsuratkumar, a beggar-saint from south India, who died in February 2001. These intimate sharings, the legacy of Lee's dangerous prayers, are contained in several volumes, published only by request of his teacher: *Death of a Dishonest Man* and *Gasping for Air in a Vacuum*.[3]

Lee called his own poems "bad poetry" and that is exactly what they are—sort of in the way the blues is bad in comparison to a classical sonata. His words are the outpourings of one man's enormous love, enormous pain and enormous longing. The fact that these prayers are published, and in such quantity, was never Lee's intention. Rather, in much the way that the bluesman had no choice but to moan his tune as a cry to heaven, Lee's words erupted from his own longing and ecstatic heart. He needed a form with which to communicate the overwhelming nature of his obsession, his love for God in the person of his master. He picked up his pen.

Jelaluddin Rumi did the same thing in thirteenth century Persia, and the Hindu saint Mirabai did it in the fourteenth century in India. Each of these mystics produced a phenomenal body of work, and all of it spontaneously rendered. Over 30,000 verses are credited to Rumi, who sang his life in relationship to his beloved master, the Shams (Sun) of Tabriz. Over 5000 songs in praise of the Dark One, the Lord Krishna himself, are credited to Mira. In neither case did the poet set out to publish or impress a public in any way. Theirs was a poetry of the bedchamber, a whispering of love; or a poetry of the interior castle in which the poet, like a servant, bowed reverently as he offered words of adoration to the king or queen of his heart.

Both Rumi and Mira are bad poets, then, in the sense that they are uncensored. Their hymns and rants flow like lava from a soul on fire. Renegades and heretics they were too. Rumi violated the protocol of an academician, sending his students away so that he might devote his attention solely to the mad beggar, Shams, whom he recognized as his Beloved of all ages. Rumi's words are not polite, especially when he rails against the empty form of much religious observance. His "sister" Mira was a rebel too. She refused to sleep with her prince husband, knowing herself to be wed to Krishna from childhood. Mira would be satisfied with no worldly accoutrements. Her only consolation lay in the sound of Krishna's flute; her only security was in knowing that she had nothing but the eyes and smiles of her dark-skinned Lord. Lee Lozowick, a similar renegade and heretic, wrote mystical prayers with one hand, rock and roll lyrics with the other.

Lee probably argued that Rumi's or Mirabai's poetry was good while his was still bad, and so did a few contemporary critics. But, one who reads him at any length might very well argue back that the expressions came from the same chamber of the heart in which Rumi and Mira lived, and for that they are invaluable to the hungry seeker, the man or woman who wishes to dive deep in the ocean of prayer. In the genre of spontaneous, untamed art, which nevertheless communicates objective truth, Lee Lozowick's bad poetry/ bad prayers will, I assert, stand the same test of time that Rumi's and Mirabai's have.

Praying my teacher's poetry, as I do, I am immersed in the realm of dangerous prayer—in fact, I must admit that the whole notion of praying dangerously arises from this source for me. His poetry taken as a whole is actually a textbook on prayer for anyone who cares to study the subject. However, the various chapters of this text only reveal themselves over time—a study that would be well worth the effort. These chapters might be called "The Practice of Ruthless Honesty Before God," "Constancy of Attention," "Crediting All Things to the Source of All," "Stoking The Sweet Fire of Longing," "Praise, Praise and Only Praise," and "Gratitude in Everything," to name a few. More dangerous still, the same man who instructed his students to not implore God for favors as if they lacked anything, unabashedly used his poems to beg gifts constantly from his own master. Ah, but what favors did he ask for? In answering that one question we touch upon the nerve in the root of dangerous prayer. Lee Lozowick's poems to his master, Yogi Ramsuratkumar, are nothing less than pleas for complete annihilation in love, for madness in God, for death to all that would separate him from his Beloved, and paradoxically, for the grace of non-union—a mysterious request whereby the mystic relinquishes the satisfaction of merging so that he or she can still worship the Beloved. Merged as one, who would be lover and who Beloved? Or so reasons the intoxicated heart! Such a request for "love in separation" is the cry of a fool.

Lee Lozowick was such a fool and his prayers prove it. Who else but a madman would beg for madness, annihilation, union and non-union at the same time? Yet, contradictions and outrageous requests of this nature mean nothing to a drunken, love-intoxicated fool. If one day his heart is moved to celebrate the eternal identity of God and human, that becomes his form of prayer for that day. If the next day he feels the throbbing pulse of separation, that becomes his prayer. On another day, God is beyond our reach—the ultimate, the transcendent Absolute. A few hours later, God is heralded as closer to us than the breath of our own lungs. Since when has love ever demanded logical consistency? Since when has love ever followed a map? Lee Lozowick admitted his ignorance of theology or even his facility for lofty sentiments. Like a candle flame, all he knew was to burn.

The prayers of this mad lover are invitations to us who read them to kick up our own heels a bit. What's holding us back from our own brand of spontaneous, honest, even wild and mad communication with God? Lee proved to us, his students, how available these sentiments are, and how fearful we are to express them. One day, as we gathered to study the teaching, he invited us to write our complaints of longing to God. He indicated that these complaints were not about the weather or about our old model car, but about our inability to grasp the ineffable, our inability to find God in all things, our desires to have our hearts ignited. This form of prayer is actually a reputable and acknowledged form, known as *nindaa stuti*, or ironical praise, in Indian literature. It is the form in which many great lovers have praised the Beloved, speaking of this One as cruel and heartless, because the Beloved has kept them in separation. In using the language of complaint, the writer or "pray-er" is actually offering a type of praise unique and intimate to his or her relationship with God.

In the writing exercise that Lee guided us in we hesitated. Still, he encouraged us. "Just write it down. Don't worry about the results. Just start," he was like a coach. "Everybody can do this. It's simple. It's all in you already, you just have to get going and the words will write themselves." And write we did, for twenty minutes or so without stopping. When he called upon us to share some of what we'd written, we were amazed. People who had never written a poem or a prayer before were reading lines that left the rest of us in tears. Lee had made his point, and with startling clarity. All we needed was the space of possibility—the permission to write the worst poetry in the world—leaving the results to God. This is exactly the mood of risk-taking and abandon that characterizes praying dangerously. We dare to pray our real heart's desire, we dare to admit our own foolishness, we dare to ask for something we are totally unprepared to receive, because somewhere in our hearts we know that this is what we were created for. We disrobe before God, and we dance.

So You, Madman,
    is this one of Your celebrated Sins?
You have broken lee's heart
    and now You break his mind?
I will not run from You
    for are You not my Father?
In fact I will sacrifice myself willingly
into Your equally willing embrace.
Yes, oh dirty Beggar,
    I am beyond tests and trials.
You are making Your son
    as Mad as You.
lee throws himself headlong
    at Your dusty Feet
and thanks You for crushing him
    until there is nothing but You.
You make the sweetest wine
    of very sour grapes.

                      (July 24, 1994)[4]

We too need madness. We don't have to look far to see that what the world calls madness is really our only sanctuary, the only condition in which we will ever find satisfaction. Let's face it, it is mad to ask for God, knowing that our ego-run lives will be ruined as a consequence. It is madness to ask to serve others, and forever, knowing that we will never be thanked, but rather rejected and criticized in the process. It is utter insanity to live a life of simplicity, rejecting the values of a culture that judges our worth on our financial portfolios and the cut of our clothing. Such is the madness of the prophets who, throughout the ages, have stood up in the marketplace or in the courtyard of the palace and cried out, "Hey, what are you guys thinking? Have you all gone mad?"

> For so long I sought riches,
>     and found much wealth
> till I discovered You,
>     a Beggar,
> and now seek only the Poverty
>     You so regally bear.
> To be as Poor as You,
>     Beloved Guru,
> is a blessing I only dream of
>     with awe.
> So sings Lee, his wealth effaced
>     in the Poverty of his Lord.
> May this only be so.
>                                     (Winter 1981) [5]

## 4. Gurdjieff on Prayer

Lord Creator, and all you His assistants, help us to be able to remember ourselves at all times in order that we may avoid involuntary actions, as only through them can evil manifest itself.
—Gurdjieff, quoted in *The Struggle of the Magicians*[6]

The importance of G.I. Gurdjieff's work in the spiritual orientation of our times is unquestionable to anyone who has studied his teaching even cursorily. Yet, for those who haven't, his name, if recognizable at all, may evoke little more than a vague association with some unsavory and suspicious methodologies, perhaps with the connotation of dark magic. The association is understandable, as people tend to condemn whatever threatens them or to discredit what is unfamiliar. Gurdjieff was a dangerous man. His methods were designed to shock people, to rub against the grain. In a time when scientific knowledge was fast replacing the ancient traditions, Gurdjieff boldly served up a hard, cold lump of reality to twentieth-century men and women, telling them that they were "asleep," that they were "machines," and that they had no soul unless they built one.

In one sense Gurdjieff's teaching was about leaving the translational domain of petitioning prayer and entering into the transformational domain of aligning with the Absolute, which he described as "attuning with the Logos ... "[7] He indicted us all, saying that we cannot pray authentically because we do not know ourselves—we are fragmented individuals, with so many conflicting thoughts, desires, urges and addictions. One part of us (one "I") prays for help, while another "I" continuously undermines the help that is given, and so on.

This distinction about numerous "I's" is central to Gurdjieff's teaching. He taught that we have multiple internal voices or internal points of view, separate "I's" all vying for dominance. The preeminent example of the lack of integration of the "I's" being that we set the alarm clock at night with one "I" fully intending to get up early, but when it rings another "I" turns it off and rolls over. Without an integration of all the multiple "I's" into one singular "master," a person's fate is that of a horse-drawn carriage racing out of control. The mind (the "driver") is disconnected from the body (the "carriage"), and both are being carried away by the emotions (the "horse").

Along these lines, Gurdjieff taught that three forces are at play in every circumstance. There is the affirming force, the "I want"; there is the denying force—"I do not want"; and there is the reconciling force that stands between the tension created by this constant battle between yes and no. Who or what commands that reconciling force is what marks the difference between mechanical life or conscious existence.

Furthermore, Gurdjieff noted that we lack the trained attention required for such a dynamic process as true prayer. We start with our focus on prayer and fifteen seconds later we are planning our dinner menu. And, perhaps most serious of all, we pray mechanically, saying words that we are not willing to live. If we really felt, knew and acted such words with our whole being we would be radically transformed, and so would our religions and our world.

To make a long and complex story very short, Gurdjieff was born in Armenia around 1866 and died in Paris in 1949. He spent his youth in an environment that included exposure to both ancient traditions and modern science, and as a young man set out upon a search for the truth. This search took him to monasteries and schools of esoteric knowledge in Central

Asia and the Middle East for a period of over twenty years. As James Moore describes in his biography of Gurdjieff:

As a youth his precocious visits to Echmiadzin [the holy city of the Armenians] and the monastery of Sanaine had presaged long journeys: seeking in Cappodocia the origin of Christian liturgy; in Mount Athos the legacy of Hesychasm; in Jerusalem the link with the Essenes; and in Coptic Abyssinia the roots of Christian Gnosis.[8]

What he learned from these immense and intense journeys influenced the work with others that he began in Russia around 1912. In 1919, after perilous encounters that marked his exit from a revolution-torn Russia, he landed in Constantinople where he founded his formal organization, calling it The Institute for the Harmonious Development of Man. And after that, he settled in the Paris area in 1922 with the same Institute.

From 1922 until his death in 1949, Gurdjieff worked both in Europe and in the U.S. with small groups of serious students, including a handful of brilliant writers, scholars and musicians. His ways of working gained him a reputation for being both a genius and a reprobate, as he often shocked people from their normally mechanical ways of being to convince them of their sleeping condition. Gurdjieff knew that only with an experiential reference point to one's mechanicality and condition of sleep—their unconscious habitual behavior—was it possible to have the motivation to work on self. Only with such motivation could one learn to trust something other than the internal voice that urges safety, convenience and the status quo. And this voice is only one of numerous "I's" that run the human being, keeping him or her in a constant state of disintegration and hence confusion. In his book about his early life, *Meetings With Remarkable Men*, Gurdjieff wrote:

> I wished to create around myself conditions in which man would be continuously reminded of the sense and aim of his existence by an unavoidable friction between his conscience and the automatic manifestations of his nature.[9]

Gurdjieff wrote three masterworks, and left a huge legacy of his teachings in the people who had studied with him and who continued to disseminate his work throughout the world during his lifetime and up to this day. As to his major theme, the idea that we are "asleep" is certainly not a new one to most of us. Most contemporary spiritual and psychotherapeutic movements use such terminology. But, in this day of easy answers to difficult questions, the notion of awakening from that sleep is often made synonymous with some momentary insight into the nature of reality, some peak experience—an experience that we have all had, many of us as children. It is easy to create these momentary breakthroughs in the short term, as evidenced by the enormous popularity of the spiritual and psychotherapeutic workshops that have swept the Western world in the last thirty years. Such glimpses, however, provide a short-lived high. In contrast, living from the context of awakening, moment to moment and day in and day out, is generally not our daily bread. We might be able to talk a good line for a while, or show up with blazing insight when circumstances push us up against the proverbial wall, but when conditions settle into life *as it is* we are distracted by every bauble that drifts across the horizon, the TV set or the computer screen. We do not observe ourselves enough to know "the terror of the situation," as Gurdjieff called it—the recognition that everything about us is mechanical; that we interpret and speak and act entirely out of habit; that everything about us is committed to maintaining the status quo. Despite what the great religious traditions have told us for centuries—that we must die to the old self to awaken as a new self—we don't want to die and will do everything to avoid it. Even if we accept the theory that transformation is about death and resurrection, dying is not something that we accomplish in a weekend workshop.

Awakened from pure mechanicality (sleep), Gurdjieff taught that a man or woman was enabled in building a soul, and thereby establishing a conscious relationship to the Absolute. Without a soul, or some inner matrix built by intention and attention, how could man or woman possibly hold and channel the energies of heaven? How could man presume to attract God's attention if that same man showed himself completely untrustworthy by his constant dissipation of the energy that he was attempting to accumulate? It seems to me that all efforts against this dissipative tendency, all efforts in the direction of building a soul, or establishing this matrix of attention and intention, are nothing less than prayer.

Gurdjieff delineated that the human is a four-centered being—that we each have a thinking center, a feeling center, a moving center and an instinctive center. We hear such terminology as "head, heart and gut" bandied about in every discipline today. Yet, few are the resources that would grant us some means of integrating these centers. Gurdjieff did that. He saw the central dilemma and great tragedy of modern civilization as being the over emphasis on the thinking function to the neglect of the feeling and moving functions, and to the discouragement of any possibility of integration of the human being to their rightful place in the process of evolution.

According to Gurdjieff, furthermore, all contemporary culture merely reinforces in us the illusory notion that we are conscious beings, rather than automatons. After all, don't we have more choices than ever in our gourmet health-food supermarkets? After all, don't we have the Internet by which to connect people from all different religious faiths in one great equalizing cyberspace? It is difficult to face the illusion of sleep when we live in the city that never sleeps; or when we run ourselves ragged with all kinds of diversions and all kinds of obsessions after money and things, fueled by Starbucks. All our enormous scientific and technological accomplishments merely fill up our waking and sleeping hours, reducing any possibility of making use of the space and time in our lives when we are aware of who we are and where we are headed and what we might be building, ultimately. Thus, even as we gain enormous amounts of data about our universe, we lose our hold on personal relationship, to ourselves as well as to others. We are undermining the human possibility, the possibility of moral power, will and intelligence, by our numerous diversions into the novel, the chic and the perverse. There is no hope for such men or women to integrate their centers, and beyond that to render themselves as individuals who can actually return something of value to life in the way of participating in the conscious evolution of the species.

One of the most radical (and encouraging) aspects of Gurdjieff's teaching was that this work on self could take place in the midst of ordinary life; that what had previously been reserved to a chosen few in some monastery, could now be the lot of any person, regardless of life circumstances or responsibilities. However, the work he offered had to be practiced to the extent that it informed one's entire life, even in times of chaos. One must practice on the battlefield, literally, as Gurdjieff himself instructed his students to practice as they left Russia in the midst of revolution. They were also taught to be invisible to the rest of their countrymen.

One of Gurdjieff's first students, P.D. Ouspensky, in his book *In Search of the Miraculous*, noted that toward the end of 1916 Gurdjieff spoke several times about religion, particularly about Christianity. "No one has a right to call himself a Christian who does not carry out Christ's precepts,"[10] Gurdjieff said. In response to these assertions, Gurdjieff was asked if prayer could help a person to live like a Christian (in this case), to which he replied that it depended upon "whose prayer" it was. If the one who was praying was the ordinary, subjective man, he would use his prayer for subjective results alone, "namely, self-consolation, self-suggestion, self-hypnosis."[11] No objective results would ever accrue from this type of prayer.

In speaking of a particular type of true and objective prayer, Gurdjieff drove home another point saying: "In Christian worship there are very many prayers ... where it is necessary to reflect upon each word. But they lose all sense and all meaning when they are repeated or sung mechanically."[12]

This mechanical approach to ritual is precisely the excuse that many modern people offer for their break with the religious traditions of their childhood. Yet, how many of those who have left the church have incorporated a genuinely conscious, non-mechanical prayer into their own lives? It seems a convenient strategy of ego to justify its own mechanicality by projecting it on the official church, or the priest per se.

Elaborating, Gurdjieff said:

Take the ordinary *God have mercy upon me!* What does it mean? A man is appealing to God. He should think a little, he should make a comparison and ask himself what God is and what he is. Then he is asking God to have *mercy* upon him. But for this God must first of all *think of him, take notice of him.* But is it worth while taking notice of him? What is there in him that is worth thinking about? And who is to think about him? God himself. You see, all these thoughts and yet many others would pass through his mind when he utters this simple prayer.[13]

The idea that God will notice those with a soul, with some receptive environment and some ability to work with what God is offering, is a radical and even repulsive notion. We want to believe that God is all compassionate and will keep coming back to our door, even when we have broken our vows ten thousand times, as the Sufis say of the Beloved's persistence. While I think Gurdjieff would not argue with this, he is paradoxically offering a practical teaching that grounds our idealistic notions of what kind of effort it takes to be able to hold and make use of the Beloved's grace.

*And then it is precisely these thoughts which could do for him what he asks God to do.* But what can he be thinking of and what result can a prayer give if he merely repeats like a parrot: "God have mercy! God have mercy! God have mercy!" You know yourselves that this can give no result whatever.[14]

"Result" is not to be understood in usual terms as some material accumulation—like getting a new job or better car, or being healed from some disease. The "results" of prayer of this type would be entirely in the domain of refinement of the instrument, the human power of attention, such that it might become more usable to the process of evolution. In waking up, then, the human fulfills his genuine purpose in life and is thus able to take his place in the scheme of creation, a place that has been closed to him not by God's whimsy or power, but rather because he simply could not endure in such a rarefied environment without having prepared himself for the task. One is reminded of C. S. Lewis's famous tale in which everyone starts off in heaven after death, but most eventually opt to live in hell because heaven's grass is so real that it cuts the feet, while hell's roads promise comfort. The road to hell still invites illusion's slippers.

Another passage about prayer in Gurdjieff's cosmology comes from a more contemporary source, written in 1969 by Irmis Popoff, an American woman who began as a student of Ouspensky's and then studied and worked with Gurdjieff himself for many years. Irmis was a Catholic by birth and the subject of prayer and of religious life in general was of great interest to her. As she kept detailed journals of her interactions with G., she recounts here a view of prayer that is coincident with another core element of G.'s teaching, that of the accumulation and storing of energy for work on self. This passage touches upon the idea of tapping into the shared prayer of the devout throughout the world, and of using this energy, for a time at least, to accomplish one's own work.

This energy that Gurdjieff refers to, however, is not loaned out free of charge. In borrowing from this bank one knowingly obligates oneself to some payback, and with interest. Gurdjieff here calls the payback "conscious efforts" (and "intentional suffering"—a concept too complex and open to misunderstanding to explore here). By conscious efforts he alludes to a primary tenet of this teaching, that one must always do more than they can. The next leap in the evolutionary cycle could not be accomplished without such efforts.

Reading this passage, I am further impressed with the upward-drawing power that it communicates. One *feels* a certain necessity for an erect posture, the possibility of linking these energies of heaven with those of the earth, the alchemical alignment that make for prayer.

Irmis writes:

I understood Mr. Gurdjieff to tell us once, at the Wellington, that all people who pray and believe in a finer, higher life release a great deal of energy when they pray. It was then that he mentioned that it would be most useful for us to think often about this kind of energy; to imagine it arising from the earth to the upper regions, as high up as our thoughts could reach, trying to direct them to some point well known to each one of us, way up in heavens—a group of stars, a constellation, anything. To imagine all this energy, originating from all believing humanity past, present, and future, reaching this place above and becoming concentrated there. To this unknown place in outer space we should then direct our thoughts and, wishing with all our hearts, we should feel that we were charging ourselves with this energy thus released and accumulated by lofty aspirations from all directions of the Earth; that we were storing it for the purpose of working on ourselves so that it would help us to grow into "men made in the image of God. And having done that," he added, "promise yourselves that you will pay back for the energy you have stolen, through conscious efforts and intentional suffering, when the time comes for you to pay."[15]

Following these brief passages, then, we can summarize Gurdjieff's approach to prayer as being a call to fully inhabit our own being, and thus to be in relationship with higher forces. That full inhabitation requires a constancy of vigilance, a paying of attention, a remembering of self. Like Jesus's words to his disciples in the Garden of Gethsemane, Gurdjieff is inviting us to "Watch and pray with me," a job that Jesus's disciples failed at miserably. In the next essay, about Simone Weil, we will further explore this "prayer by attention" that Gurdjieff pointed to throughout his work.

## 5. SIMONE WEIL ON PRAYER

The need for the training of attention was paramount in the prayer cosmology of mystic and philosopher, Simone Weil (1909-1943). In her spiritual autobiography she recounts a practice that bears a strong resemblance to the kind of focused attention that Gurdjieff was speaking of in his comments about prayer. Of her time in working in an agricultural colony in the south of France, Simone wrote:

> I recited the Our Father in Greek every day before work, and I repeated it very often in the vineyard ... Since that time I have a practice of saying it through once each morning with absolute attention. The effect of the practice is extraordinary and surprises me every time. At times the very first words tear my thoughts from my body and transport it to a place outside space where there is neither perspective nor point of view. The infinity of the ordinary expanses of perception is replaced by an infinity to the second or sometimes the third degree. At the same time, filling every part of this infinity of infinity, there is silence, a silence which is not an absence of sound but which is the object of a positive sensation, more positive than that of sound ... Sometimes, also, during this recitation or at other moments, Christ is present with me in person, but his presence is infinitely more real, more moving, more clear than on that first occasion when he took possession of me.[16]

For Weil, this ability to focus one's attention and direct it toward God was the very substance of prayer. Directed toward the other, it was the substance of love. She wrote:

... prayer consists of attention. It is the orientation of all the attention of which the soul is capable toward God. The quality of the attention counts for much in the quality of prayer. Warmth of heart cannot make up for it.[17]

In her essay entitled, "Reflections on the Right Use of School Studies with a View to the Love of God" she appealed to adolescents and their teachers (in the 1930s and '40s) to set their studies within a context of preparation for a higher purpose—that of prayer—rather than as the ticket for good marks, to pass exams or to win academic successes. Imagine trying to give that context to our kids today when we ourselves don't have it? Impossible! For that reason, Simone Weil's insights into this subject of attention may be of use to us, adolescents that we are in the domain of the spirit.

Weil was a brilliant student herself. She graduated from her normal school, a sort of college equivalent, first in her class ahead of all the men in the class, with her friend Simone de Beauvoir in second place. She lived a radical and revolutionary lifestyle, apprenticing herself in situations of extreme stress (working in a Renault factory during the war, 1934-35, and joining the Spanish at the front of the revolution in their country in 1936) in order to learn about human nature first hand. Her writings run the gamut from political treatises and revolutionary calls to action, to exquisite theological apologies on the value of suffering in the life of the soul.

What is of interest here in our consideration of dangerous prayer is that prayer, in Simone's view, took effort of attention and that attention could be gained in a variety of means. If we are to delve deeply into prayer in our own lives a similar shift of context is obviously called for. Is it possible for us, like the teenagers to whom she wrote in the 1930s, to reassign our daily affairs as preparations for learning attention? Can we clean the bathroom with attention, watching our thoughts, our breathing, our extraneous efforts? Can we eat our solitary lunch in this way? How about attending to the filing of papers on our desk? Or raking the garden? If it is not possible to keep attention throughout these activities, it is at least possible to set intention at the beginning of an activity. But how often do we take a moment to remember as we move from one job to the next, from one room to the next, from one phone call to the next? The whole preparation for prayer is just that ordinary ... and that difficult. When we see how lacking in attention we are, it should actually be cause for great celebration. To know that we have no attention is the first step in moving toward it.

We can start learning attention by looking at those common activities that potentially dissipate the attention that we have already accumulated. Such forms of dissipation might include TV-watching, reading material that simply distracts us into fantasy, or putting energy into relationships that are insipid and dead-ending. Such self-examination is dangerous stuff, however. It means that to be a man or woman of prayer, as Simone Weil would hold this for us, we might have to exercise discipline and courage in the face of cultural ennui. The point to keep in mind here is not that these activities are bad or immoral. Rather, they are simply ways that drain energy that might be better spent in getting us closer to what we say we really want—a one-pointed focus on the Divine.

Not only did Simone Weil call us to attention, she also offered us some help in what attention meant. Far from being a kind of militant pushing, a straining of the will, the attention that attracts the Divine would be feminized. It must be soft attention. It must be the attention of the lover. Holding-our-breath type of attention doesn't cut it where relationship or prayer is concerned. What Simone Weil suggests is an attention of receptivity, in the mood of waiting upon God:

> Attention consists of suspending our thought, leaving it detached, empty, and ready to … receive in its naked truth the object that is to penetrate it…. All wrong translations, all absurdities in geometry problems, all clumsiness of style, and all faulty connection of ideas in compositions and essays, all such things are due to the fact that thought has seized upon some idea too hastily, and being thus prematurely blocked, is not open to the truth. The cause is always that we have wanted to be too active; we have wanted to carry out a search … We do not obtain the most precious gifts by going in search of them but by waiting for them. Man cannot discover them by his own powers, and if he sets out to seek for them he will find in their place counterfeits of which he will be unable to discern the falsity.
>
> In every school exercise there is a special way of waiting upon truth, setting our hearts upon it, yet not allowing ourselves to go out in search of it. There is a way of giving our attention to the data of a problem in geometry without trying to find the solution or to the words of a Latin or Greek text without trying to arrive at the meaning, a way of waiting, when we are writing, for the right word to come of itself at the end of our pen, while we merely reject all inadequate words … Every school exercise, thought of in this way, is like a sacrament …[18]

It is clear, however, that while waiting is called for, such waiting is not mushy. In fact, this feminine approach to practice really requires discipline and vigilance to carry out. The waiting is focused, full of attention and intention. This is why our prayer life is such a challenging adventure. We learn the ways of prayer as we learn the ways and means of attention, and that often takes a lot longer than we would like. But, for those who are serious in their desire for a life of prayer, the fact that we can practice attention in every activity of life and thus build the matrix of prayer more strongly, should be heartening news. To make every activity a prayer, to make every moment a sacrament is what we are here for.

## 6. PRAYING WITH THEIR BLOOD: THE DANGEROUS PRAYERS OF DANIEL AND PHILIP BERRIGAN

As of this writing Daniel Berrigan is still alive. His brother Philip Berrigan died in 2002. As Daniel ages it becomes safer to speak openly and write about the two of them as heroes, calling them true mystics, prophets, martyrs even, and ultimate disciples of their master, Jesus Christ. Their works are included in anthologies, in social treatises and in books on prayer. As more time passes, when the spell of our current malaise of mystification with the computer terminal and the good life has broken again by terrorism, or an incident or two of nuclear and military madness, we may remember these men even more. As we recall their voices that cried out unceasingly, out of love for us, we may grieve more deeply.

While they are alive, the Berrigans and others like them who pray dangerously, offering their own blood as a witness of their love for God and humanity, make us uncomfortable. While such prophets are immediately demanding a metanoia, a real transformation, it is hard to listen with an open mind and heart. While their courageous actions and long-suffering endurance of prison and deprivation niggles at our conscience, we readily deny these terrifying implications to our own sedate and comfortable spirituality.

Time wears the edges off the discomfort we feel at such crazy wise behavior and such examples of radical reliance on God. Like the great and tormented lovers, teachers, poets, prophets and saints before them, the Berrigans too will be consigned to the shelves as icons to be nodded at. Out of sight, if not out of mind, they will be manageable and safe.

Throughout my life I have been awakened from complacent

sleep by the voices of Daniel and Philip Berrigan, and for that I am enormously grateful. In this spirit of gratitude for the gnawing discomfort and profound inspiration they have effected for me, I offer this tiny testimony to their dangerous prayer. Perhaps my readers will join me in the admission of their own discomfort in the presence of such surrender to God, and join me in welcoming and embracing this discomfort as a doorway to truth.

None of us who lived in the U.S. through the 1960s and '70s, and who prayed and marched for peace, protesting America's involvement in the Vietnam War, was ignorant of the radical outlaw Roman Catholic priests, Daniel Berrigan, a Jesuit, and his younger brother Philip, then a member of the Josephite order. In 1968, these men and seven other supporters poured their own blood on and set fire to draft records in Baltimore and Catonsville, Maryland. "The Catonsville Nine" as they came to be called were an embarrassment to many in their church hierarchy, an enigma to God-fearing people throughout the world, and an outrage and a threat to the proponents of the military-industrial complex.

For the Berrigan brothers, prayer demanded action. "We were simply doing what faith demanded of us," Philip would say of this time. And Daniel would write:

Our apologies good friends
for the fracture of good order
the burning of paper instead of children
The angering of the orderlies in the front parlor of the
    charnel house
We could not, so help us God, do otherwise,
for we are sick at heart
Our hearts give no rest for thinking
of the land of Burning Children.[19]

Sentenced for the destruction of federal property, they served two-year terms in the Danbury, Connecticut prison. Once released from incarceration, however, their zeal for witnessing to the truth amidst the growing insanity of war was multiplied rather than restrained. Forming a network of communities known as Plowshares, they commenced their active resistance phase in September of 1980, when, with six companions, the two brothers walked into the General Electric Missile Re-entry Division in King of Prussia, Pennsylvania, and hammered missile nose-cones, and poured blood on top-secret missile engineering drawings.

The pattern established in this first intervention has served as a prototype to dozens more direct-action protests that Plowshares has taken responsibility for to this day. The inspiration and directive for their work is drawn from the book of Isaiah in the Old Testament scriptures in which God speaks to Isaiah of the work of the days to come when:

The Lord God will settle disputes among great nations.
They will hammer their swords into plowshares
and their spears into pruning knives.
Nations will never again go to war,
never prepare for battle again." (2:4)

Using the same instruments, like the hammer and the saw, that humankind has used for millennia in the construction of shelter, participants in Plowshares' actions assault the ultra-technological weapons of mass destruction. Of course their attacks are insignificant in effecting damage of any serious nature. Warships and missiles are built to withstand the most extreme conditions, and they know this; they are not fools. They splash their own blood, drawn prior to the event, to symbolically represent the wanton loss of human life, the terror and the tragedy that such weapon-machines systematically enact. The activists make no attempt to escape when apprehended, rather they choose arrest, confinement, trial and imprisonment as their participation in the suffering and crucifixion of Christ on behalf of humanity. Herein lies their contribution and their dangerous prayer.

Daniel and Philip Berrigan (and those before and after them, Mahatma Gandhi, Martin Luther King, Dorothy Day ... innumerable others) were more than libertarians, freedom fighters or social activists. Rather, they were (and are) warriors of God. Armed with prayer and the grace of their devotion, and grounded in contemplation of the words and example of Christ, or Buddha, or the great saints and prophets of their tradition, such men and women are literally burned alive from within with the outrageous love of God. Yet, such love is not a platonic affair for them. Theirs is a love that must be shared; and for those whose calling is to witness, it is a love that must be bled. Unlike the once-active passion for the truth that has quelled in many hearts, theirs is a love that hasn't faded or grown sterile or complacent with the years.

In the year 2000, at the age of 77, and only two years before his death, Philip Berrigan was still praying with his blood, sitting in prison in Maryland for actions against the A-10 planes, delivery systems for depleted uranium munitions (U 238). Depleted uranium is a radioactive alpha-emitter and a chemically-toxic heavy metal. Shot at the men, women and children of Iraq, it also destroys the environment and the health of our own military personnel, testimony once again to the insanity and immorality of war. At Philip's trial, however, the federal government would entertain no expert testimony on the effects of U238.

"We're all going to die in a world that is worse than when we entered it," remarked Daniel Berrigan in an interview in 2000. "The depth of the death urge, and the extent of it day after day in the world is just simply appalling, it stops one short … [Yet,] the good is to be done because it is good, not because it goes somewhere."[20]

Daniel's point, which he applies to his life as a poet, priest and teacher as well as to his risks as a protestor, is that when there is purity in an action—when the need to receive approval or notoriety or personal merit is out of the picture—it *will* go somewhere. "I believe that with all my heart, but I'm not responsible for its going somewhere." In other words, one simply does the work that is presented, surrendering the results to God. Berrigan elaborated:

Gandhi … insist[ed] that soul (soul force is what he called it), was the main issue. Spirituality was the main issue. Connection with God was the main issue. And if that were the main issue, the issue of tactics would fall in place … We'd all like to see the fruit of our labors, but biblically speaking I'd almost say that there's some kind of a mysterious law operating in this way that the more serious the work to be done the less one will see of the outcome … And so you have a very interesting measuring stick about serious work. And that's very hard. I mean this business about peacemaking, its tough, unfinished, blood-ridden, everything is worse now than when I started, and I'm at peace. I don't have to prove my life. I just have to live.[21]

How one prays in the midst of hell and yet remains at peace is not a blessing casually earned. Writing of her experience in Ravensbruck, the notorious Nazi death camp for women, Corrie Ten Boom wrote:

Life in Ravensbruck took place on two separate levels, mutually impossible. One, the observable, external life, grew every day more horrible. The other, the life we lived with God, grew daily better, truth upon truth, glory upon glory. Sometimes I would slip the bible from its little sack with hands that shook, so mysterious had it become to me. It was new; it had just been written. I marveled sometimes that the ink was dry. I had believed the Bible always, but reading it now had nothing to do with belief. It was simply a description of the way things were —of hell and heaven, of how people act and how God acts ... [22]

The Ten Booms, the Berrigans and their like have practiced, studied, prayed and prepared their bodies, their minds and their hearts for the inevitable imprisonment that their actions lead to as they attempt to appraise us all of our sins. For it would be utter foolishness to think that their protests are meant solely for the warmakers at the Pentagon. We are all warmakers—whether we kill our children's spirits with stupid and cruel words; whether we fill our homes with grandiose toys made at the expense of the poor; whether we simply sit by and lend no support to the pleas of our prophets and saints who are calling us to awaken from the darkness around us.

We should be bothered by the Berrigans. It was their vocation to make us uncomfortable. Their prayer, in the witness of their lives, should cause us to reexamine our mediocrity of purpose and intention. Their prayer should get us up in the middle of the night and push us out of bed in the morning to carry on the vocations—to fulfill the destiny—to which each of have been called.

Let us pray dangerously. Let us face squarely the sullen satisfaction of life in the new millennium. Let us listen to the uncompromising voice of the spirit within us, as the Berrigans listen to the scriptures. Let us remember what we are here for. Let us pray.

X

# Praying on the Subway

Transit states are particularly potent times for prayer, and not simply because travel in buses, on subways, by air, or in our cars at high speed or in slow traffic can be annoying, stressful or even dangerous. As any type of travel moves us from one place to another, one domain or realm to another, it prefigures the really big transitions or changes of state of everyday life—like birth, death, transformation or loss. A subway ride across midtown, for instance, can be an ideal venue in which to practice dying. The metaphors are numerous: both involve a passage, and perhaps through a tunnel, and both involve us in darkness. Imagine the benefit of using a daily subway ride with the intention to recapitulate your life's work, to pray for all who have served you; to prepare yourself with sharpened attention for your final stop.

I've done a fair amount of airplane travel in my work, and I always note that there are men and women who study the Bible or read the Koran as they fly. Maybe like me they're just white-knuckle travelers who are doing their best to keep from panic, to prevent themselves from running up the aisle of the plane screaming "we're gonna crash" at the first signs of turbulence. But I don't think so. I think that many people in this world do orient their lives around God's word, and I am awed and humbled to see this. A large airplane or a crowded bus or train presents me with a wide cross-section of humanity, and

I get to see what others are up to. I also get countless opportunities to practice kindness, generosity, compassion and the offering of merit on behalf of all.

And speaking of praying while traveling ... the best story I've ever read on the subject, which was related as true, was about a business man (let's call him Joe) flying home from Chicago after a long conference. Joe found himself on the plane situated next to an empty seat. Hoping to keep it that way, he spread out his carryons and coat to discourage the last passengers boarding from choosing this spot. When everyone was apparently settled, and the seat remained unoccupied, he realized his great good fortune, and breathed a sigh of relief. Before the doors were closed, however, the steward announced that they were holding the plane a few minutes longer to accommodate two additional passengers making a tight connection. Cursing slightly under his breath, Joe made a prayer of sorts, something like, "Oh God, please give me a break here." And with that, two women dressed in white entered the plane amid a great hubbub by the pilot and crew who greeted them. As the women at last bustled their way up the aisle, Joe was astonished to recognize Mother Teresa accompanied by another sari-clad nun moving toward him. And then she stopped, smiled at him and directly pointed to this empty seat. With no mind at all, Joe immediately stood to give her entry, as her companion moved on to find another place.

As the plane taxied down the runway Mother Teresa took out her rosary and quietly fingered it, while Joe, still stunned, kept respectful silence. Still, he couldn't help but notice that her rosary was a bit unconventional. Each set of ten beads (known as a "decade") was a different color—red, blue, yellow, and so on. Finally, as the plane reached its cruising altitude, and unable to suppress his curiosity any longer, he remarked to the elderly nun about her unusual rosary. Without apology she told him that she liked it because it reminded her to pray for the whole world: on the red beads she might pray for the continent of Europe, on the blue ones for Africa. In this way, her prayer was never limited; her intentions were always for all. Needless to say, Joe, a former Catholic, was touched and impressed with her story, and soon they were discussing this and that.

When Mother Teresa asked him if he prayed the rosary, Joe candidly admitted that he had long since left behind his connections to both church and ritual prayer. She was undiscouraged. Taking the colored rosary from her pocket she handed it to him, urging him to use it once again. And with deep gratitude he accepted this priceless gift.

As the story goes (and I won't guarantee that it may not be somewhat apocryphal), Joe left the airplane in a new frame of mind and, with a healing of heart, once again began to pray the rosary.

Not long after his return home, Joe was confronted with the shocking news that his beloved sister had been diagnosed with terminal cancer. Interestingly, his first response was to take hold of the saintly woman's rosary that he carried now all the time, and to pray for his sister. Then, hurrying to meet her, he handed over the special rosary, telling her the amazing story and expressing his faith that this prayer would not fail to be useful to her. And apparently it was. Joe's sister used the rosary faithfully throughout her treatment, and successfully overcame the illness. Then, she passed the rosary along to another friend in need. And so the prayer continues; who knows where it is today ... maybe Mother Teresa's rosary will make its way to one of us some day. Prayer like hers alters people's lives. It also obviously kept her own transformational work alive!

## ALTERING LIVES

Praying in transit is a bit like reverse terrorism. Instead of intimidating and threatening the other passengers on this bus, we become pacifists, quietly offering peace and blessings invisibly to those around us. Prayer in mass transit, or any prayer in crowded public places (like on the city streets, in concert halls or conference centers, in schools, in church on a busy Sunday morning) tends to interfere with a usual preoccupation in "my" little world—where I alone am the shining star. When others are visible to me, their pain and their need can become obvious if I am willing to open to it.

The motivation to pray is everywhere, in every face, pleading through every word. That man who shouts through his cell phone disturbing all around him? Isn't he crying out for God's attention? I don't mean this condescendingly, but rather as a sincere wakeup call to myself. I too need help. I too am desperate to be heard. If I can remember that *he is me*, my prayer for him and with him arises immediately. If I can remember that he and I are both missing the mark—in the sense that we forget our organically innocent condition—I can use this reminder to fall into a place of forgiveness and to soften my hold on controlling what is. I am then in prayer.

Praying in transit can be as simple as a gentle gaze up and down the length of the train car or airplane with an internalized blessing or inward smile as you confide each person there to the benevolent hands of the Divine Mother, recalling that it is the Mother's good pleasure to give everything to her children. Certainly you want to be invisible in the way you do this, except in clearly safe circumstances, as your eyes and smiles might be misinterpreted with some serious consequences to you. What this type of prayer has done is to move you aside for the time being and to place the needs of others first.

If you have a particularly favorite prayer or name of God, or a revered mantra, the repetition of this on behalf of each person on your flight, or everybody in this same audience with you, could be a way to generously inspire yourself to increase the prayer's use for the glory of God as well as for the merit that might somehow be applied to your fellow pilgrims.

Some people look exceedingly troubled as they ride public transportation. Others look zoned out with i-Pods attached. Certain people look mean and threatening. And these designations based on appearances may or may not be true. "It ain't necessarily so," as the song goes. I've been surprised by joy, finding the tattooed and tenderhearted Harley rider ready to come to my assistance, and I've been shocked by the language of judgment coming from a priest or rabbi. Still, hard and judgmental, zoned-out, scary, anxious are the ways some other people protect themselves from more pain. The more they impress me, the more they may need my prayers. The only question is, am I up for it? Am I willing to embrace the world, full of the wounded, and me a part of it?

We may never know how our blessing or prayer affects the life of another. Really not our business, after all. But one thing is certain, we will know this prayer's effect on our own lives. Touched by compassion, I am transformed.

## OUT OF CONTROL

Mass transit is dangerous to ego because it involves giving up control. Even to take the same old bus to the same old supermarket you must leave your familiar home; you must put yourself in the hands of a driver other than yourself. *You* are not in charge of the route, the speed, the cleanliness or attitudes of the other passengers. *You* are thus at the mercy or the whim of forces you cannot control, even if you wanted to. Occasionally you will be exposed to new and sometimes terrifying stimuli. Doesn't this sound a lot like dying or at least as an opportunity to build your inner life? Seems to me that the only relevant issue is whether or not I will conduct myself with dignity and good humor through this transition, even if terrifying thought forms and emotional monsters are raging. Now that prayer as dignity would be a form worth practicing—to take my transport seat as my deathbed and to practice equanimity, focus, re-affiming my aim.   How would I conduct myself from a hospice bed if my morphine drip wasn't working properly? Would I berate my beloved caregiver; would I call my lawyer and start suing somebody? What about using whatever pain, discomfort or confusion I have as a way to unite with others who suffer in a similar way throughout the world? How about living and dying with dignity and nobility?

Not long ago I was visiting New York City, coming home late in the evening on the N train in route to the R which would take me to Brooklyn. Taking my seat near the door I had entered, I wondered why this most convenient seat and several around it were left open. Then I looked across the aisle toward the other door. Nauseated, I saw a sizeable load of human turds, obviously fresh, immediately in front of the entrance. It was perfectly placed so that if someone was not highly observant as they stepped into the subway car from the station platform, they would land right in it. And that is just what happened. Before I could get his attention, a young orthodox Jewish man, his black clothing and side locks of hair setting him apart from the crowd, had stepped there, both to my horror and to his. He sat down, much disturbed, and was mumbling something under his breath as he looked at his filthy shoe. I reached into my purse and took out every old paper napkin and tissue that I had (I'm a collector of such things) and went to him with an offer of assistance. He refused. Then, I took the napkins and covered the shit pile, hoping this would alert other incoming passengers of its presence. It worked. At the next stop people getting on the train walked around the suspicious "something" and didn't look back.

I tell this story a bit because I'm proud of my courage in that moment, which isn't always my strong suit. I had a lucky moment in which I was more concerned for others than for myself. But I tell the story primarily because it drives home the point that praying in transit teaches me that I am always in the right spot to pray. There is no place where God is not; there is no other moment except this one in which our love can be expressed. Even in a shit-filled train car I'm in the temple, if I remember to use it that way. And what great practice for dying! I think we might have to encounter a lot of such shit in the land of last resorts. Dying isn't antiseptic. War is hell. Horrors abound. Every day offers us ways and means to pray that won't always involve incense, candles and saints in white robes. Dignified prayer in transit, yes. I remember. In this moment, whether I'm feeling resistant or not, feeling devotional or not, prayer can characterize my life.

## AWAKE AT THE WHEEL

We were stuck in traffic on I-5 outside of Seattle. The signs told us that the backup was six miles long. I was pissed. "Okay," I jokingly remarked to my husband and my friend Nancy who had picked us up at the airport, "I suppose I could use the time to pray. I am working on an essay about prayer in transit, after all." My husband kept the mood light, inviting me to admire one gorgeous pine tree. Still, projecting myself into some imagined time and place that was better than right here, right now, I resented the delay. *Ah well.* So much good material for self observation gets served up on the road.

If you are like me, you spend a lot of time in your car, generally driving, but also as a passenger. And I wonder how many of us overlook this extraordinary chance to pray. I'm talking about prayer beyond just a little "God bless our trip" sort of prayer. The car is a sealed chamber, and that's no small gift. If we can avoid the radio or the music CDs for a while, we just might tune into some new channels of communication that we didn't know existed before.

We just might transform a predictable and apparently boring task of simply getting someplace else into a pilgrimage, a process, a period of practice. What if the getting there with dignity and remembrance was the real work? What if we used the time to simply attune to our breath, knowing it as the breath of God. Or to breathe with tenderness toward ourselves and others? What if we used this chance to have a heart-to-heart talk with God? What if we practiced remembering and resting in the Presence, despite all evidence to the contrary? What if we sang the psalms or chanted with vigor, or created our own Litany of the Road in which we spoke the name of someone we loved, or someone we had a big problem with, or someone in power, or someone in need, and followed that naming with the invocation "Lord have mercy." Can you see how the possibilities are endless?

I drive forty miles each way to get to my teacher's ashram. I make this trip at least four times a week. I listen to tapes of great books, I listen to my guru's voice speaking some aspect of his teaching, and I also pray, bringing myself present to what is, where I am, how my posture aligns. I use the time to reassert intention. I might use it to contemplate a particular point that I read in a book or a question that arose in my morning mediation, like "What is kindness, really?" Posing oneself a question is a great way to pray. Sure beats worrying about what to make for dinner. And even that can be transformed into prayer.

The great thing about praying in transit, whether in the car or by mass transit, is that you tend to arrive at your destination with renewed intention, even if you are physically tired. To step out of your car after a half hour of prayer is great preparation for whatever follows, whether that is a doctor's visit, a sojourn at the grocery store, or rendezvous with your kids or other loved ones.

At the same time, we must stay particularly alert to what we do with ourselves as we drive. Praying in the car, then, can be a way to test our level of alertness and genuine presence in prayer. So much that is associated with prayer has a dreaminess associated with it. Maybe because we love to pray in candlelight, with the hypnotic drone of Gregorian or Sanskrit chant in the background. Maybe because we saw in others a gentle and delicate look as they prayed, or because we saw tears in the eyes of those in ecstasy.

For me, it is important to guard against any sentimental overtones that might be associated with prayer. I easily get as attached to and dependent on prayer beads as I might to a new pair of gold or diamond earrings. Spiritual materialism easily triumphs, and that includes my attachments to a degree of warm fuzziness in prayer.

The prayer that is truly dangerous, prayer that is transformational, is sharp and clear, even if it is surrounded by chaos, confusion or distraction. The man or woman who prays dangerously is awake at the wheel, alert to the hypnotic pull of the white line that might draw him or her into drowsiness.

For this reason I'm a little skeptical of these courses in awareness that have you chewing every mouthful of food fifty times, and walking with attention to heel-ball-toe at every stop. Certainly these are lovely practices to do on retreat, or to simply keep in mind as you must run to catch your bus. Dignity, dignity, dignity... But if your prayer is to radically alter your life, and the lives of those around you, it needs to be bright prayer, not dreamy fantasy-enriched enthrallment with emptiness.

Real emptiness is razor sharp. Reality is sharp. That's why they call it *real*. C.S. Lewis tells a great story about the residents of hell who take a bus trip to heaven, with the clear understanding that if they truly like it better there they can elect to stay. The unfortunate "damned" pack the bus, but when they get to the Elysian Fields they are thwarted at every turn. The grass blades actually cut into the flesh of their feet, and every step becomes a painful ordeal. After only a brief sojourn they flock back to their bus, relieved to be going back to the comfort of their illusions, an apt description of life in hell. Heaven is simply too tangible, sensual, sharp, hard. Heaven is too real. And so is life on the road, racing along an interstate at 70 mph, or navigating through a city at rush hour.

I urge us all to wake up our prayers and wake up ourselves. I urge us to be conscious participants in prayer, giving bright, alert praise and thanks and supplication. I urge us to pray as adults with bodies and heightened senses, not as displaced spirits. I vote for praying dangerously.

Pray outdoors. Hang your feet over the edge of a cliff, or
    sit on a precarious limb on an old tree, and pray.
Balance on one foot, or stretch your arms into a cross,
    and pray the prayer of all the fools for love who
    have preceded you.
Stand under a cold shower or drink a stiff Scotch and
    watch the mind dissolve or put on rock and roll
    and dance until you collapse, and give up trying to
    protect yourself from being tired.
Get down on the floor and play with your child, and
    don't get stodgy. Be silly in your prayer and in your
    play.
Or make wild love to your husband or wife and use
    laughter as your aphrodisiac. Pray!
Jump up and down fifteen times, or pinch yourself, or
    send your heart around the world in the blink of
    an eye. Pray.
Now look into the face of a dying friend even as you
    look into the mirror seeing yourself die. Pray.
Stay there forever and pray for the whole of creation to
    be happy, at peace and aware of its Buddha nature.
It's a good beginning.

                                   —RSR

# XI

# WRITING OUR PRAYERS

There seems a connection between the pen and the heart. Many writers know this, although we certainly can't prove it scientifically. Something about the pure act of creation— starting from the nothing of the clean, empty page; moving the hand that holds the pen across the emptiness and inscribing it with our revelations, our dreams, our secrets. Ah, where there was nothing, now there is something. What a miracle!

When I write slowly, moreover, I find that the words seem to sink more deeply into my being. "Contemplative writing," others have called it. Sometimes that writing breaks out spontaneously into prayer. I might be describing the environment, noting the force of a summer rainstorm here in the high desert, when suddenly I am overwhelmed with awe, unable to express what I see except as a paean of praise or gratitude to beauty, or truth, or goodness.

In India, at the ashram of my teacher's master, I observed several Indian devotees sitting with notebook and pen, writing throughout the master's *darshan*, which often lasted for two hours or more. They were writing a mantra, a phrase that contained one of the many names of God, filling page and page with it: *Om Sri Ram Jai Ram, Jai Jai Ram,* and each inscription was done with meticulous care, never rushed.

ॐ श्री राम जम राम जम जम राम

I imagined that such a practice must be intolerably boring, as I recalled the punishments for misconduct in grade
school, writing out five hundred times: "I must not chew gum
in class." Over time, however, as I gained greater appreciation
of the ways and means by which one can keep one's focus on
God, I learned that such writing could be a tremendous act of
contemplation.

Within the self-help movement, and even in business
seminars, it is often standard procedure to write out state-
ments of positive regard or affirmations of one's goals: "I am
likable, lovable and creative." Or, "I easily close this and every
deal." The more senses one involves in the process of learning,
the greater chance one has of maximizing memory retention
and gaining positive results. Repetition and reinforcement
convince the nay-saying voices in our minds that they are
outnumbered and overpowered. In the domain of our prayer,
writing my prayers and seeing the words I've written, and listening to myself say the words slowly, both as I write them
and after I complete them, is an aid to opening up the meaning contained within the words. Such writing goes straight to
my heart. I am prayer-writing. I am praying in much the way
a temple dancer or a choir singer combines body, mind and
heart in her offering.

To write a short phrase of prayer, or to copy a favorite
prayer repeatedly, has the potential to be an extremely pure
act. It is a meaningless, holy waste of time. We waste our time
in writing the praise of God as there is no one to approve this
activity, and nothing meaningful to show for it. We do it for
no good reason.

We sometimes don't know what we know, or how much we know, until we are called upon to answer for it. I didn't know how much I knew about prayer until I took on the task of writing this book. And, while our prayer life certainly doesn't require that we write a book, writing a prayer or two might be a revelation. Living in duality, as we do, I think we would be foolish not to use every means at our disposal to give us what we say we want.

Writing my prayer inspires me to pray more. It also helps me to clear those areas of the spiritual path where brambles of uncertainty are temporarily blocking the way. Sometimes as I write about an issue I am amazed at the clarity that emerges. I actually get someplace; I understand something I didn't think I understood before. At other times, writing leaves me circling around my doubts and fears or frustrations, offering no way out. In those times, writing is extremely helpful. I simply leave a sentence unfinished, and on the next line I write an offering—a prayer—of my confusion and uncertainty, giving it all back to God; acknowledging my own helplessness. The writing has inspired prayer.

## FATHER THEOPHANE'S MESSAGE

I only met Father Theophane once. He spoke at a retreat in the Colorado mountains, not far from the Trappist monastery at Snowmass where he lived at the time. Theophane the monk was an unforgettable person. Well over six feet tall, thin as a willow, wiry, but with no sharp points. Theophane's presence was that of a crazy-wise man. He exemplified the injunction of his master, Jesus, that "unless you turn and become as little children you cannot enter the kingdom of heaven." At the same time, there wasn't naiveté in his playfulness and innocence. Theophane gave the impression that he could see in many directions and in many dimensions all at once, and I was drawn to him immediately.

I was even more drawn to him when I read his book, *Tales of a Magic Monastery*, which I number among the classics of contemplative prayer of our day. Once read, Theophane's *Tales* is the type of book you want close at hand for the rest of your life. The type of book that invites itself into your luggage on long trips. Filled with simple stories, all of them reported to be true, it is written in a mythic, mystical genre that challenges the logical mind. Yet, like the great Zen stories or the parables of the fathers of the desert of early Christianity, each one offers a koan of sorts that begs to be worked with until a tiny doorway to understanding, beyond mind, shows itself. The book is a feast.

One of the most helpful stories for me, and one that should serve our purpose here, is called "Write My Own Bible." The narrator of this tale is a man who has made a yearly retreat at the Magic Monastery for forty years. On his very first visit he forgot his Bible, and so asked the guestmaster if he could borrow one. A simple enough request, one would imagine. But, as the guestmaster was a man of wisdom (probably Theophane himself, since that was his job for many years), he responded in a completely surprising way.

"Wouldn't you care to write your own?" the guestmaster asked the retreatant.

The man was dumbfounded, so the guestmaster explained:

"You could tell of a classical bondage and the great liberation, a promised land, sacred songs, a messiah— that kind of thing. Ought to be much more interesting than just reading someone else's Bible. And you might learn more."[1]

Despite his incredulity, the man took the monk's suggestion and spent his weeks on retreat writing his own Bible. The
guestmaster then recommended that he take this Bible home
with him, make it the foundation for living over the next year,
and keep a journal, recording his successes and failures, his
insights, his prayers.

The narrator reports that he followed the monk's suggestions
to the letter and found for himself more life and energy in relat-
ing to his own Bible than in any official Bible he had ever used.
Moreover, the man said, "my daily meditations had never been
so concentrated."[2] When a year had passed, the man journeyed
back to the Magic Monastery for his next retreat, carrying his
own Bible and his journal with him. After a few days, the guestmaster gently instructed him to consign his two precious books
to the flames, which he did. All that effort, all that great insight,
now up in smoke! That done, the monk suggested that the man
begin again, that he use his retreat to write his own Bible.

The narrator concludes:

> And so it went, these past forty years. Each year a new
> Bible, a new journal, and then at the end of the year—
> into the flames. Until now I have never told anyone
> about this.[3]

Who knows, perhaps today is the day he burns the results
of last year.

## Writing Your Way Home

For many years I've been conducting journal-writing workshops that I have called "Writing Your Way Home." Journal-

writing has long been a popular topic, and the interest in writing grows as more and more people take up some practice via blogs or other social media. Almost everyone I know does some form of writing for themselves. We write to clarify our emotional issues, to express our grief, to keep account of the good times and the bad, to vent our frustrations, to encourage our creativity, to tell the world what we think. In my experience, however, I find that a lot of us write predominantly about our psychological processes, validating our feelings and opinions, and miss taking the next step, which is to use our writing as an access to the essence of being, or to that which lies deeper than our psychology. Writing can be an access to the heart of God. As such, writing is potentially a powerful means of prayer.

Most of us write from the context of psychology. If you don't keep a journal it may be for that very reason, that you simply use up your lovely notebook with an endless series of self-doubts, internal dialogues to try to boost your flagging spirits, unbreakable circles of insights that look great but change nothing, and lists upon lists of complaints, to name but a few of the boring diatribes that I find creeping into my journal writing when I'm not being careful, paying attention and remembering. When I sit down to write, therefore, I often feel that I have nothing to say that bears being expressed.

The context of psychology is a context of functionality, reflecting back to the distinction between translational religion vs. transformational religion as we considered it in the Introduction. The context of psychology is a valuable and necessary one. Because we are human, sometimes it helps to relieve our stress to write about our feelings. It's not that I'm saying to put it all away. But, since we're considering the subject of praying dangerously I would simply invite you to explore more deeply. As far as I've plumbed this ocean, I've seen that most of our journal writing and Internet postings arise from the context—the firmly held belief system—that we are separate from God, that we are ignorant of the truth, that we are victims of circumstance, and that all the stuff that "happens" to us in our daily lives really makes a difference. Most writing flows from the notion that our thoughts are important, that our emotions have credibility, that our memories and past experiences dictate our futures, and that by putting these illusions into form, by the use of words in our book or in emails to friends, we somehow make them holy, inviolable and valid. None of which is true. In fact, since we do tend to reinforce our illusions by speaking and writing of them as if they were real, we may actually be undermining and disempowering our intention for communication and communion with the real.

When such illusions are refused, far from causing us to repress our feelings and become cold-hearted and rigid, something entirely different may emerge. A new being may be conceived, nurtured and grown in the writing that uses essence as its lover, rather than mind.

At first, the participants in my workshops are troubled by my suggestions of another approach. What will they write about now that I've asked them to eliminate reflections on psychological processes? Up until now their opinions about things, their emotional turmoils or exaltations, their endless reports of failures and successes may have provided continual fascination. They may have the impression that, with enough reportage, they might finally arrive at some solution to the great dilemma in which they find themselves—namely, how to get the love they think they lack. When I suggest that a shift of context is in order, from one of a scarcity of love and of interesting things to write about, to one of abundant love, basic goodness and no end to writing about the wonders of the spirit, some of them are thrilled. Others, tentative. A few, still remain terrified. No matter, a few hours later they are all writing like mad, wondering how they could have missed the obvious for so long.

To "write one's way home" is to use writing to remember what one already knows, and to keep using writing that puts this remembrance in the forefront, whatever the circumstances of life around us. The point is, everything that occurs is prospective food for our prayer life. Therefore, everything that occurs can be written about from a perspective that honors essence. What we do when we write our way home is to re-frame or re-contextualize life's occurrences in the light of prayer. For example, instead of complaining about things, or delving into the reasons that such things are happening to us based in the past, based upon our upbringing, we assign such things in writing to the hands of God. Isn't that exactly what King David did throughout his great songs of agony and ecstasy, which we call "the psalms" today? "Out of the depths I have cried unto Thee, O Lord. Lord, hear my prayer. Let Thine ears be attentive to the voice of my supplication" (psalm 130) David wrote, thousands of years ago.

And I continue today, using my own words,

If You, O Lord, were looking only upon my failings and my sins, I wouldn't have the stupidity to call upon You. But, I know that is not what You are.

You are the God of merciful forgiveness. And how I need You when my own mercy is so thin, my own forgiveness so shallow.

You are the God of my strength. I can't seem to muster enough from this poor physical body to endure much beyond this hour. But, despite my weak faith, I know that Your strength is available to me—through the breath, through the holy Name, through the touch of this friend, through the remembrance of You. Come to me. Assist me in this time of struggle. Show me what is real, and dispel my illusions.

Writing our pain as prayer is only one of a dozen different ways to transform a journaling practice into a means of igniting the inner life.

## WRITING ONE TRUE SENTENCE ABOUT PRAYER

On September 4, 1998 I wrote an entry about prayer in my journal using a technique I had learned from an essay by Ernest Hemingway about "writing one true sentence" at a time. What that means for me is to write only what is true in my own experience, rather than what I've read about or heard about and would like to think is true, and would like my listeners or readers to think that I know about, even though I haven't lived it. It is a method of thoughtful writing in which I allow the sentence just written to gel properly, at which time the next few "true" words start to emerge, naturally forming another true sentence as an extension of or in addition to the previous one. This kind of writing is not concerned with filling up a certain number of pages or with writing as fast as I can write, both of which can be valuable techniques to generate creative expression. On the contrary, writing one true sentence at a time can be a sort of Bible-writing, as Father Theophanes's guestmaster might have spoken about it. Herein one records the truth of God, as God has revealed God's-self to one soul.

This is what I wrote that day:

Somebody around here [me, of course] should write a book about prayer, since the market can't seem to get enough of them. In the meantime, however, I'm inspired this morning to put down some thoughts about the subject to determine if I know anything that might be worth communicating. So, here goes attempt #1.

## About prayer

Regina has been praying since the time she was a child. That's over fifty years of praying now! Like the progression of spiritual life, prayer started off being self-centered and evolved to being more "for" others. That same evolution can sometimes be seen within one short meditation period, one short prayer time. It starts off as something she "does" and evolves to being something that "is done," in and through her. It is no longer precisely correct to say that "Regina prays." Certainly she puts herself in the posture of prayer, and she invokes (somedays it feel like she "dredges up") remembrance and intention. But what actually occurs doesn't seem like the act of an individual in the process of supplication, or even in the process of thanksgiving or adoration. What seems to occur is that the physical form, the body, becomes enlivened somehow. She has dared to say, "it becomes enlivened by the Divine," because she doesn't know what else to call this sensation of overshadowing or sense of Presence that often accompanies prayer. It seems that the Divine itself prays. Regina just happens to be there, some vehicle or an instrument or a voice, or whatever, for that prayer ...

And so on I wrote. A few "true" paragraphs later, I felt like maybe I could write this book after all. I also found that giving words to my inner experience was helpful, I had clarified something for myself, and for a moment or two I knew what I knew. I was also struck with a sense of gratitude to the source of that knowledge.

\* \* \*

What do you know about prayer? What do you know about the source of that knowledge? What are you sure you *don't know* about prayer? Or, what are sure is *not true* of prayer, or not true of God, since it is sometimes easier to come at such things through the back door, especially since many of us have bad associations with such religious concepts. But, all that past stuff aside, and all that I've written aside, and all that you've ever read about prayer or God aside, and all judgement and doctrine aside, when have you tasted prayer? What circumstances invite prayer, or invoke prayer, or inspire you to pray?

Why not write about prayer? As you write, however, I suggest that you avoid backsliding into diatribes about the negative impressions you received about prayer from Sister Mary Annunciata or Father McMurphy. Or the feminist platform you stood on in college, rebelling against your rabbi and the men in the synagogue who exiled the women to the balcony during prayer services. I suggest that you ignore for a while any other story from your past that gives you another illusory excuse about why you can't or don't pray more dangerously now. Leave those stories for your other writing projects. They make fabulous novels.

In the domain of writing about prayer I suggest that you stay with what you know and don't know in the present, without blame or explanation, without self-judgment or criticism of others. I believe that the urge to prayer is a pull in the heart that can actually be strengthened by hardship, even refined by misdirection, and certainly deepened by the desire to know what is genuinely true in contrast to all that has been proscribed or taught, which never really felt like God or prayer anyway, when you come right down to it. And, coming right down to it is the point of such praying dangerously. Staying present to what is, as it is, write that!

## TAKING YOURSELF OUT OF THE PICTURE

Prayer may certainly be one of the most personal and intimate experiences that any of us will ever have. Yet, the great mystics often confound us with the impersonal nature of their prayers as much as they do with the almost erotic sensuality of their writing about God. This paradox is integral to the relationship that prayer engenders and expresses. We come to God thinking we are separate, individual, and God makes us aware that we are and always have been one with God. Never separate. In that realization there is an inherent sensuality, sometimes even an explosion of sensuality, not unlike the merging of energy fields, of bodies, that happens when sex drives us out of our separation-making minds. My teacher has playfully and wisely used S-E-X as an acronym. "Suddenly, Ego, eXits," he points out. And the same is true when we are praying dangerously. The "I" that entered into prayer is absorbed into the Eye of the Beloved, the Sufi mystic might say. Rumi's words are, "He drove me out of myself."

As a method of discouraging identification with personal experiences, as if they were somehow special or unique to us,

I recommend doing some journal-writing in the third person, using "she" or "his," or using your own name instead of "I" or "my" or "me." You'll remember that I did this in the selection from my journal in the last essay. While it may have sounded a bit strange at first, and for some people definitely challenges romantic notions of what the journal is, the practice is one of the most helpful methods I've ever used. And many of the participants in my seminars will verify the same. Writing about spiritual life without the use of the personal pronoun engenders a different focus and forces issues to surface that you may never have known you had like your attachment to "your" vision. Primarily, though, such writing creates the smallest wedge of space between the experiencer and the experience itself. A wedge that can be used vitally to help us from solidifying the identification we normally have with our experiences. We believe that we are defined, and therefore limited, by what goes on in and around us, and certainly by our judgements and evaluations of those experiences. We believe that our take on circumstances is the only possible interpretation. We easily get lost in our illusions, tied as we are to attachments and desires. When we write about such things as if they are happening to this friend named Regina or as "this woman" with her insight, we gain the tiniest fraction of objectivity in the situation. The strangle-hold of identification is loosened, and we get a precious breath of distance from our own minds. Such practice helps when used over time. When we change the words by which we refer to the workings of the mind, and when we take that valued step back, away from absolute identification, we slowly but surely instruct the unconscious mind in a truth it needs well to learn. We are helping ourselves establish a habit that will be tremendously useful when the mind is struggling for dominance in a situation of panic or chaos. We get to watch it, rather than be swept up into its insane cycle of negativity and fear.

"Taking Yourself Out of the Picture" has another meaning as well. I also use this phrase as an invitation to write a prayer that is largely non-self-reflective. There is a time and place for prayer that offers my needs and requests, and even *my* love. But, a prayer that focuses on God first, me second, holds a different promise. Here, for instance, we might compose a litany of gratitude for the beauty of creation or the awesomeness of God's power. We might use our prayer writing to invoke some particular face or aspect of the Divinity for the sake of the world—like the sword of Kali, or the tender mercy of the Divine Mother. If we have a teacher or spiritual master, living or dead, our prayer-writing might focus on praise of his or her kindness, gentleness, wisdom—objectively, not simply in relation to us. We might also write about the aspects of God as these are reflected in those around us—praising God through honoring the simplicity and innocence of children; celebrating a man or woman we admire as a reflection of God's fidelity, generosity or attention. The point is not that you never mention yourself, the point is to move beyond yourself as separate, as singular, as unique. Praying for others, or on behalf of others, is another way to do this, provided you steer clear of any tendency to collect do-gooder points in the process.

## WRITING A DEATH PRAYER AND OTHER SPECIAL PRAYERS

In many non-traditional marriage ceremonies today it is common practice for the partners to design their own service and to write their own vows. Standing in front of the gathered family and friends, and generally nervous, the bride or groom will typically unfold a small paper on which they have written their prayers. Looking into their partner's eyes, often choking up with sentiment, these very personal promises are then recited aloud. When such vow-writing is taken seriously, as one would hope it is as a part of the marriage ceremony, it can be an extremely powerful means of defining what marriage means, and invoking the help of those present, as well as the help of the deity in whose name the vow is made.

Ideally, marriage represents a death to ego, and is itself a dangerous prayer in which two people promise to put themselves second to the love that has brought them together. With the growing divorce rates, among non-traditionals and traditionals alike, one could only wish that such vows might be laminated or framed and placed somewhere in the house where the couple would read them, regularly, renewing even on a daily basis the mood and the intention they held on their wedding day. Perhaps such recollection might make a difference in the way men and women treated one another. Unfortunately, however, we seem to take our vows lightly when ego wants to be served.

My teacher has written a few prayers over the years that he has shared with his students. He has given us a meal prayer, a travel prayer, a birth prayer, a marriage vow and a death prayer. Contemplating these regularly I find an endless source of inspiration, and committing them to memory I therefore have at my disposal a tool that can effect an immediate shift of context in any situation. Standing at the dinner table, often still hassled by the day's labors, the meal prayer calls me back to the reflection that this food is the very substance of the Divine, given for my nourishment. The death prayer has been applicable not only in relationship to a physical death, but to all the small daily deaths that one encounters on the path of *sadhana*.

Regardless of whether you have access to such prayers composed by others or not, I recommend the process of writing your own prayers, at least for special occasions. Such prayers need not be carved into stone, but rather considered as trail markers that keep you on course. They can be revised, frequently. To write the kind of prayer that you would wish to have on your lips at the moment of death is a task that brings you face to face with important issues that bear examination on a regular basis, like the nature of impermanence.

Books filled with other peoples' prayers, or favorite prayers from throughout the centuries, are extremely popular these days. Some of them are genuinely inspiring. To spend a quiet hour or more, meditatively reading the words of scripture or the prayers of others, may be an invaluable source of contemplation. But ultimately, to read others' prayers is only as effective as we make those words our own. I suggest that we try writing our own prayers once in a while as a means of strengthening our intentions, clarifying our longing, celebrating that voice which is ours, giving form to the sentiments of our own hearts.

How would you ideally like to pray in your first conscious moment of the day as your rub the sleep from your eyes? In other words, what prayer would you like to characterize the orientation of your soul throughout the day ahead? Well, why not try writing that prayer. Or writing a prayer for the conclusion of your day. Or a prayer for driving around town doing errands, like a "Walking Through the Mall Prayer." Or a prayer for starting the preparation of a meal. Or a prayer to say before putting the kids to bed. Or a prayer of dedication of your lovemaking with your partner. The possibilities of course are endless. Even writing this list has reminded me of occasions that I would like to sacramentalize more formally by composing a prayer about them.

Like the suggestion to write your own Bible, I recommend that you write "Everywoman's (or Everyman's) Book of Common Prayer," simply for the fun of it. That means, write your prayers regardless of how simple and unliterary the expressions may be. In fact, the criteria for writing good prayers is honesty, as in writing "one true sentence," not exalted language or poetry. One of the loveliest and most honest prayers I know—a prayer for invoking the Goddess Tara—was given to author China Galland by a Nepalese renunciate. It begins like this:

Alas, I do not know either the mystical word … nor do I know the songs of praise to thee, nor how to welcome thee, nor how to meditate on thee … or how to inform thee of my distress. But this much I know, O Mother, that to take refuge in thee is to destroy all my miseries.[4]

Along the same lines, the prayer of one blind man who approached the master Jesus, begging for a healing (Mark 9:24), admitted his poverty of faith when he prayed, and dangerously: "Lord I believe, help Thou my unbelief."

# ENDNOTES

## Chapter 1: Transformational Prayer

1 Goethe, "Holy Longing," translated by Robert Bly, in *News of the Universe, poems of twofold consciousness*, San Francisco, Sierra Club Books, 1980, p. 70.

2 Weil, Simone, *The Simone Weil Reader*, George A. Panichas, editor, New York: David McKay Co., p. 417.

3 Wilber, Ken, quoted in: *What Is Enlightenment?* "A Spirituality That Transforms," Fall/Winter 1997, p. 25.

4 Rumi, *We Are Three*, trans. by Coleman Barks, Athens, Ga.: Maypop, 1987, p. 12. Used with permission.

5 Kabir, *The Kabir Book*, versions by Robert Bly, Boston: Beacon Press, 1971, 1977 by Robert Bly; © 1977 by the Seventies Press, p. 25. Reprinted by permission of Beacon Press, Boston.

6 *The Cloud of Unknowing and Other Works*, trans. by Clifton Wolters, New York: Viking Penguin, reprinted 1978, p. 68.

7 In *Daughter of Fire*, Nevada City, Calif.: Blue Dolphin Publishing, 1986, p. v.

8 Rumi, *Crazy As We Are: Selected Rubais from Divan-i Kebir*, Nevit O. Ergin, translator, Prescott, Arizona: Hohm Press, 1992, p. 5. Used with permission of publisher.

9 This phrase was used extensively by Zen Master Suzuki Roshi, whose book, *Zen Mind, Beginner's Mind* (New York: Weatherhill, 1970) stands as a classic in the field of Zen studies.

## Chapter 2: Starting From Nowhere

1 Eliot, T.S., *Four Quartets*, "East Coker," section III, lines 123-128, New York: Harcourt, Brace, Jovanovich, 1943, p. 28. Used with permission.

2 See: Hillesum, Etty, *An Interrupted Life: The Diaries of Etty Hillesum, 1941-43*. New York: Washington Square Press, 1985, and *Letters from Westerbork*. New York: Pantheon Books, 1986.

3 Trungpa Rinpoche, Chögyam, *Cutting Through Spiritual Materialism*, Boston: Shambhala Publications, 1973.

## Chapter 3: A Cosmology of Praying Dangerously

1 Ten Boom, Corrie, *The Hiding Place*, New York: Bantam Books, 1971, p. 238.

2 *See:* Heschel, Abraham J. and Samuel H. Dresner, *I Asked for Wonder: A Spiritual Anthology*, New York: Crossroad / Herder and Herder, 1983; and Steindl-Rast, David, *Gratefulness, The Heart of Prayer: an approach to life in fullness.* New York: Paulist Press, 1984, p. 9.

3 In the teaching of Lee Lozowick this phrase is synonymous with the Law of Sacrifice: "The essential nature and activity of all life, conscious and unconscious, expressed as the 'ecological' demand that life must generate new life (on many levels)." The Law of Sacrifice is the destiny of everything and

everyone. From: *Hohm Sahaj Mandir Study Manual*, Volume 1, Prescott, Ariz.: Hohm Press, 1996, p. 607.

4 Lozowick, Lee, *Cranky Rants and Bitter Wisdom from One Considered Wise in Some Quarters*, Prescott, Ariz.: Hohm Press, 2002, pp. 218-9.

## Chapter 4: Igniting the Inner Life

1 Gurdjieff's phrase "food for the moon" is presented in P.D. Ouspensky, *In Search of the Miraculous: Fragments of an Unknown Teaching*, New York: Harcourt, Brace and World, Inc., 1949, p. 85; and is found in Gurdjieff's *Beelzebub's Tales to His Grandson.* New York: E.P. Dutton, 1973.

## Chapter 5: Working with the Mind

1 The meal prayer that my teacher, Lee Lozowick, has given to us, which I use for many different occasions, includes this favorite line: "All this is Yours, for that we thank You. Even our failure to love You is Yours, for that we thank You."

## Chapter 6: The Body in Prayer

1 Tessa Bielecki's insights on prayer may be found in: *Wild at Heart: Radical Teachings of the Christian Mystics*, audio CD series available from Sounds True, 2006; *Holy Daring*, New York: Harper Collins, 1994; and *Teresa of Avila: Ecstasy and Common Sense.* Boston: Shambhala, 1996. Also see an interview with Tessa in: Ryan, Regina Sara, *The Woman Awake: Feminine Wisdom for Spiritual Life*, Prescott, Ariz.: Hohm Press, 1998, pp. 360-369.

2 Suzuki, Shunryu, *Zen Mind, Beginner's Mind.* New York: Weatherhill, 1970, p. 43.

3 Ibid., p. 44.

4 Kabir, *The Kabir Book*, versions by Robert Bly, Boston: Beacon Press, 1971, 1977 by Robert Bly; © 1977 by the Seventies Press, p. 28. Reprinted by permission of Beacon Press, Boston.

5 Lawrence, D.H., "Pax" from *The Complete Poems*, New York: Penguin, 1977, p. 700.

6 Trungpa, Chögyam Rinpoche and Sherab Chodzin, *The Path is the Goal: A Basic Handbook of Buddhist Meditation*, Boston: Shambhala, 1995.

**Chapter 7: Invisible Prayer**

1 de Foucauld, Charles, quoted in Carretto, Carlo, *Letters from the Desert*, New York: Orbis Books, 1972, p. 71.

**Chapter 8: Dangerous Prayers**

1 *Basic Goodness*, a phrase used by Chögyam Trungpa Rinpoche, is described at length in his book *Shambhala: The Sacred Path of the Warrior*, New York: Bantam, 1987. Trungpa Rinpoche says: "It is not just an arbitrary idea that the world is good because we can experience its goodness. We can experience our world as healthy and straightforward, direct and real, because our basic nature is to go along with the goodness of situations. The human potential for intelligence and dignity is attuned to experiencing the brilliance of the bright blue sky, the freshness of green fields, and the beauty of the trees and mountains. We have an actual connection to reality that can wake us up and make us feel basically, fundamentally good." (p. 31).

2 *Organic Innocence*, a term used in the teaching of Lee Lozowick, "is the basic ground of being for all manifestation, both animate and inanimate. It is context rather than content and therefore cannot be described by any particular quality. For human beings, to function from Organic Innocence is to live from the instinctual knowledge of the body, because the body is innately wise. Organic Innocence is the essential intelligence of being or existence itself as it shows up in particularized forms." From the *Hohm Sahaj Mandir Study Manual*, Prescott, Ariz.: Hohm Press, 1996, p. 618.

3 "Fourth Way" reflects the cosmology of G.I. Gurdjieff, who called his work the Fourth Way, or the way of working in the midst of ordinary life, as distinct from the three previous "ways"—the way of the monk, the way of the fakir, and the way of the yogi. E.J. Gold's book, *The Joy of Sacrifice* is published by IDHHB and Hohm Press, in Nevada City, Calif., copyright 1978.

4 Gold, E.J., *The Joy of Sacrifice*, Nevada City, Ca., IDHHB and Hohm Press, 1978, p. 146.

5 Walters, Dorothy, *Marrow of Flame: Poems of the Spiritual Journey*, Prescott, Ariz.: Hohm Press, 2000, p. 16.

6 This story is recounted by Chagdud Tulku in his book, *Lord of the Dance: The autobiography of a Tibetan lama*. Junction City, Calif.: Padma Publishing, 1992, pp. 217-218.

7 Romero, Oscar, quoted in: Brockman, James, *Romero, A Life*. New York: Orbis Books, 1989, p. 248.

8 Lozowick, Lee, *Gasping for Air in a Vacuum, Poems and Prayers to Yogi Ramsuratkumar*, Prescott, Ariz: Hohm Press, 2004, p. 666, (16 May 2002).

9 De Caussade, Jean-Pierre, *Abandonment to Divine Providence,* trans. by John Beevers, Garden City, New York: Image Books, 1975, p. i.

10 Lozowick, Lee, quoted in *As It Is,* by M. Young, Prescott, Ariz.: Hohm Press, 2000, p. 703.

11 Fox, Matthew *Sins of the Spirit, Blessings of the Flesh.* New York: Three Rivers Press, 1999, p. 46.

12 Merton, Thomas, *Praying the Psalms.* Collegeville, Minn.: The Liturgical Press, 1956, p. 12.

13 Swami Ramdas, *Thus Speaks Ramdas.* Kanhangad, India: Anandashram, 4th edition, 1969, p. 15.

14 Merton, 14.

15 "Essence habits" a phrase of E.J. Gold's to describe the trained activities that will help one in the passage through the corridor of madness when all other activities are not effective.

16 The phrase, "the Corridor of Madness," is used by E.J. Gold to describe "the period during which the psyche is 'eaten' by the essence ..." see: Gold, E.J., *The Joy of Sacrifice,* Nevada City, Calif.: IDHHB and Hohm Press, 1978, pp. 147-149.

17 "Dark Night of the Soul" is a phrase used by St. John of the Cross to describe a period in the soul's purification and advancement on the journey when all interior consolation and help seem to be absent.

18 Bhagavati, Ma Jaya Sati, quoted in *What is Enlightenment?* "don't ask why — Just Do Something," Spring/Summer 2001, p. 79.

19 Tsöndru, Yeshe, *Essence of Nectar*, Dharamsala: Library of Tibetan Works and Archives, 1979.

20 Pourjavady, Nasrollah, and Peter Lamborn Wilson, *Kings of Love*, Tehran, Iran: Imperial Iranian Academy of Philosophy, 1978, p. 38.

21 *Japanese Death Poems*, Introduction and Commentary by Yoel Hoffmann, Rutland, Vermont: Charles E. Tuttle Co., 1986, p. 117.

22 Ibid., pp. 117-8.

23 Ibid., p. 110.

## Chapter 9: People of Dangerous Prayer

1 Farid al-Din Attar. *Tadhikirat al Awliya.* Edited by R.A. Nicholson. London, 1905, vol. I, p. 73. Cited in: Margaret Smith, *Rabi'a, the Mystic*, San Francisco: Rainbow Bridge, 1977, p. 30.

2 From "The Epistle of Prayer" in *The Cloud of Unknowing and other Works*, translated by Clifton Wolters, New York: Penguin Books, 1980, p. 228.

3 Parts of this essay have been published previously in *Death of a Dishonest Man: Poems and Prayers to Yogi Ramsuratkumar*, Prescott, Ariz: Hohm Press, 1999. Used with permission of the publisher. Also see: *Gasping for Air in a Vacuum, Poems and Prayers to Yogi Ramsuratkumar,* Prescott, Ariz: Hohm Press, 2004.

4 Lozowick, Lee, *Death of a Dishonest Man, Poems and Prayers to Yogi Ramsuratkumar*, Prescott, Ariz: Hohm Press, 1999, p. 540.

5 Lozowick, Lee, *Death of a Dishonest Man, Poems and Prayers to Yogi Ramsuratkumar*, Prescott, Ariz: Hohm Press, 1999, p. 204.

6 Gurdjieff, G.I., *The Struggle of the Magicians*, Capetown: The Stourton Press, 1957, p. 47.

7 Moore, James, *Gurdjieff, The Anatomy of a Myth*, Rockport, Mass.: Element Books, 1001, p. 102.

8 Ibid., p. 76.

9 Gurdjieff, G.I., *Meetings with Remarkable Men*, New York and London: Penguin/Arkana, 1963, p. 270.

10 Ouspensky, P. D. *In Search of the Miraculous*, New York: Harcourt, Brace & World, 1949, p. 299.

11 Ibid., p. 300.

12 Ibid, p. 301.

13 Idem.

14 Ibid, pp 301-302.

15 Popoff, Irmis B., *Gurdjieff: His Work on myself...with others...for the work.* New York: Samuel Weiser, 1969, p. 146.

16 Weil, Simone, *Waiting For God*, New York: Harper Colophon Books, 1951, pp. 71-72.

17 Ibid., p. 105.

18 Ibid., pp. 111-112.

19 These words were part of the meditation spoken by Daniel Berrigan during the Catonsville, Maryland incident, May 17, 1968.

20 *RATTLE, Poetry for the 21st Century*, a literary journal, "An Interview Between Daniel Berrigan and Alan Fox," issue #11, Summer 1999, edited by Alan Fox and Stellasue Lee, p. 151 and p. 140.

21 Ibid., pp. 151-152.

22 Quoted in: Berrigan, Daniel, *Daniel: Under the Siege of the Divine*, Farmington, Penn.: The Plough Publishing House, 1998, p. 64. See: Ten Boom, Corrie, *The Hiding Place*, New York: Bantam, 1984.

**Chapter 11: Writing Our Prayers**

1 Theophane the Monk, *Tales of a Magic Monastery*, New York: The Crossroad Publishing Company, 1987, p. 43.

2 Ibid., p. 44.

3 Ibid., p. 44.

4 Galland, China, *Longing for Darkness: Tara and the Black Madonna*, New York: Viking, 1990, pp. 78-79.

# SELECT BIBLIOGRAPHY

Abil-Kheir, Shaikh Abu-Saeed. *Nobody, Son of Nobody.* Renditions by Vraje Abramian, Prescott, Ariz.: Hohm Press, 2001.

Anandamayi Ma. *Matri Darshan, A photo album about Shri Anandamayi Ma.* Westkappeln, Germany: Verlag S. Schang, 1988.

Bayrak al-Jerrahi al-Halveti, Sheikh Tosun. *The Most Beautiful Names.* Putney, Vermont: Threshold Books, 1985.

*Bhagavad-Gita.* Trans. by Sir Edwin Arnold. Los Angeles, Calif.: Self-Realization Fellowship, 1981.

Bielecki, Tessa. *Teresa of Avila: Ecstasy and Common Sense;* Boston, Mass.: Shambhala Publishers, 1996.

_____.*Wild At Heart: Radical Teachings of the Christian Mystics.* Sounds True (audio) 2006.

Bly, Robert (editor). *News of the Universe: poems of twofold consciousness.* San Francisco: Sierra Club Books, 1980.

Bourgeault, Cynthia. *Centering Prayer and Inner Awakening.* Lanham, Maryland: Cowley Books, 2004.

_____. *Mystical Hope: Trusting in the Mercy of God.* Lanham, Maryland: Cowley Books, 2001.

Carretto, Carlo. *Letters from the Desert.* New York: Orbis Books, 1972.

Chagdud Tulku. *Lord of the Dance: The autobiography of a Tibetan lama.* Junction City, Calif.: Padma Publishing, 1992.

Chagdud Tulku. *Gates to Buddhist Practice.* Junction City, Calif.: Padma Publishing, 1993.

____. *The Cloud of Unknowing and Other Works.* Trans. by Clifton Wolters, New York: Viking Penguin, reprinted 1978.

De Caussade, Jean-Pierre. *Abandonment to Divine Providence.* Trans. by John Beevers, New York: Image Books, Doubleday, 1975.

Doherty, Catherine de Hueck. *Soul of My Soul: Reflections from a Life of Prayer.* Notre Dame, Ind.: Ave Maria Press, 1985.

Fox, Matthew. *Original Blessing.* Santa Fe: Bear & Company, 1983.

Furlong, Monica. *Contemplating Now.* Philadelphia: The Westminster Press, 1971.

Galland, China. *Longing for Darkness: Tara and the Black Madonna, a Ten-Year Journey.* New York: Viking, 1990.

Gold, E.J. *The Joy of Sacrifice.* Nevada City, Calif.: IDHHB and Hohm Press, 1978.

Grabowsky, Mary-Ford. *Prayers for All People.* Garden City, N.Y.: Doubleday, 1995.

Gurdjieff, George. *Beelzebub's Tales to His Grandson.* New York: E.P. Dutton, 1973.

Hafiz. *Teachings of Hafiz.* Trans. by Gertrude Bell, London: The Octagon Press, 1979.

Hanh, Thich Nhat. *Living Buddha, Living Christ.* New York: Riverhead Books, 1995.

Harvey, Andrew. *The Essential Mystics: The Soul's Journey Into Truth,* Edison, N.J.: Castle Books, 1998.

Hillesum, Etty. *Letters From Westerbork.* New York: Pantheon Books, 1986.

____. *An Interrupted Life: The Diaries of Etty Hillesum 1941–43.* New York: Washington Square Press, 1985.

Hirschfield, Jane, editor. *Women in Praise of the Sacred.* Trans. by Jane Hirshfield with Samuel Michael Halevi, New York: HarperCollins Publishers, 1994.

John of the Cross. *Dark Night of the Soul.* Trans. by E. Allison Peers, Garden City, N. Y.: Image Books, 1959.

Kabir. *The Kabir Book.* Trans. by Robert Bly, Boston: Beacon Press, 1977.

Krishnabai, Mataji. *Guru's Grace.* 4th edition, Kanhangad, Kerala, India: Anandashram, 1989.

Llewelyn, Robert. *All Shall Be Well: The Spirituality of Julian of Norwich for Today.* Mahwah, N.J.: Paulist Press, 1982.

____. *Prayer and Contemplation.* Oxford: SLG Press, 1985.

Lozowick, Lee. *In The Fire.* Nevada City, Calif. and Prescott, Ariz.: IDHHB and Hohm Press, 1978.

____. *Death of a Dishonest Man: Poems and Prayers to Yogi Ramsuratkumar.* Prescott, Ariz: Hohm Press, 1999.

____. *Gasping for Air in A Vacuum: Poems and Prayers to Yogi Ramsuratkumar.* Prescott, Ariz: Hohm Press, 2004.

Merton, Thomas. *Contemplative Prayer.* New York: Image Books, Doubleday, 1969.

Mirabai. *For Love of the Dark One: Songs of Mirabai.* Trans. and introduction by Andrew Schelling, revised edition, Prescott, Ariz.: Hohm Press, 1998.

Ouspensky, P.D. *In Search of the Miraculous: Fragments of an Unknown Teaching.* New York: Harcourt, Brace and World, Inc., 1949.

*The Philokalia,* Boston: Faber and Faber, 1979.

Roberts, Bernadette. *The Path to No-Self.* Boston: Shambhala, 1985.

Rumi. *Crazy As We Are.* Trans. by Nevit O. Ergin, Prescott, Ariz.: Hohm Press, 1992.

Rumi. *The Ruins of the Heart.* Trans. by Edmund (Kabir) Helminski, Putney, Vermont: Threshold Books, 1981.

Rumi. *Rumi: Thief of Sleep.* Trans. by Shahram Shiva, Prescott, Ariz.: Hohm Press, 2000.

Rumi. *We Are Three.* Trans. by Coleman Barks, Athens, Ga.: Maypop, 1987.

Ryan, Regina Sara. *Only God: A Biography of Yogi Ramsuratkumar.* Prescott, Ariz.: Hohm Press, 2003.

Sen, Ramprasad. *Grace and Mercy in Her Wild Hair: Selected Poems to the Mother Goddess.* Trans. by Clinton Seely and Leonard Nathan, Prescott, Ariz.: Hohm Press, 1999.

Smith, Margaret. *Rabia the Mystic (A.D. 717–801) and Her Fellow Saints in Islam.* San Francisco: The Rainbow Bridge, 1977.

Steindl-Rast, David. *Gratefulness, The Heart of Prayer: an approach to life in fullness.* New York: Paulist Press, 1984.

Suzuki, Shunryu. *Zen Mind, Beginner's Mind.* New York: Weatherhill, 1970.

Teresa of Avila. *The Interior Castle.* Trans. by E. Allison Peers, Garden City, N.Y.: Image Books, 1961.

Trungpa, Chögyam. *Cutting Through Spiritual Materialism.* Boston and London: Shambhala, 1987.

_____. *Shambhala: The Path of the Sacred Warrior.* New York: Bantam, 1988.

_____. *Training the Mind and Cultivating Loving-Kindness.* Boston and London: Shambhala, 1985.

Theophane the Monk, *Tales of a Magic Monastery,* N.Y.: The Crossroad Publishing Company, 1987.

Tweedie, Irina. *Daughter of Fire: A Diary of a Spiritual Training with a Sufi Master.* Nevada City, Calif.: Blue Dolphin Publishing, 1986.

Vandana Mataji. *Nama Japa: Prayer of the Name, in the Hindu and Christian Traditions.* Delhi: Motilal Benarsidass, 1995.

Walters, Dorothy. *Marrow of Flame: Poems of the Spiritual Journey.* Prescott, Ariz.: Hohm Press, 2000.

*The Way of a Pilgrim.* Trans. by Olga Savin, Boston: Shambhala, 1991.

Weil, Simone. *Waiting For God.* Translated by Emma Craufurd, New York: Harper Colophon Books, 1951.

_____. *The Simone Weil Reader*. Edited by George A. Panichas, New York: David McKay Co., 1977.

Young, M. *As It Is: A Year on the Road with a Tantric Teacher*. Prescott, Ariz.: Hohm Press, 2000.

# Index

peace, 93-94, 108-110
perfection, 28, 42, 49, 141
petition, prayers of, 2, 27, 33,
34, 148, 167
Plowshares, 185
poets and poetry, "bad," 161-
166
*poornat poorna-mudachyate*, 28
Popoff, Irmis, 175-77
posture(s) of prayer, 18, 59,
63-69, 75, 176, 198, 210
power of positive thinking, 33
pride. *See*: Divine; spiritual
Prajnanpad, Swami, 75, 98
*prana*, 31
*pranam / pranaming*, 63, 65, 67
*prasad*, 67
pray, learning to, xviii-xix, 55,
151
prayer
alchemy and. *See*:
alchemy / alchemical
attempt to solve enigma
of, 71
author's relationship to,
xiv-xv
as both means and end,
63, 74-75
childish, xi, 82
communion as. *See:*
communion
constancy in, 45-48

contemplative, 37, 76,
159, 204
desire for, xix, 28-29
as expression of one's
divinity, 75
as food for God, 29-31
invisible, 76-80
as its own reward, xv, 74-
75
keeping it pure, 10-11
making it part of
everyday life, 87-88
as the most basic
relationship, 25-29, 31
motivations for, 26
place of, 52-53
of petition. *See*: petition
questions and worries
about, 17, 58-59
raw, xvi-xvii
as something done by us,
21-29
temptation to terminate,
31-35, 52
time(s) for, 49-50, 51
what it is not, 31-35
writings on, xii, 6
*See also specific topics*
prayer energy, 53, 80
prayer life, xv, 38, 45-46, 49,
53, 182, 208
building a, 47, 48

# OTHER TITLES BY REGINA SARA RYAN

## Igniting the Inner Life
by Regina Sara Ryan

This book will serve as a welcome friend to any pilgrim who wants to move deeper within. It will encourage long term but weary travelers to take that next step, and point out common detours or dead ends along this interior highway. Each chapter contains one or more contemporary poems to uplift the reader. The book concludes with suggested practices and prayers to rekindle the heart's intentions. *Igniting the Inner Life* is directed to those with a focus on spirituality, self-understanding, contemplative prayer, God, or the awakening of the heart's knowledge, regardless of the religious tradition they follow.

Hohm Press, Paper, 192 pages, $16.95, ISBN: 978-1-935387-17-6

## The Woman Awake
*Feminine Wisdom for Spiritual Life*
By Regina Sara Ryan

Through the stories and insights of great women whom the author has met or been guided by in her own journey, this book highlights many faces of the Divine Feminine: the silence, the solitude, the service, the power, the compassion, the art, the darkness, the sexuality. Read about: the Sufi poetess Rabia (8th century) and contemporary Sufi master Irina Tweedie; Hildegard of Bingen, author Kathryn Hulme (*The Nun's Story*), German healer and mystic Dina Rees, and others. Includes personal interviews with contemplative Christian monk Tessa Bielecki; artist Meinrad Craighead and Zen teacher and anthropologist Joan Halifax.

Hohm Press, Paper; 20+ photos; 518 pages; $19.95, ISBN: 978-0-934252-79-9

# Only God
*A Biography of Yogi Ramsuratkumar*
by Regina Sara Ryan

This powerful biography introduces the life and teaching work of the contemporary beggar-saint Yogi Ramsuratkumar (1918-2001) who lived on the streets of Tiruvannamalai, India. "Only God" was his creed, and his approach to everyday life. It reflected his absolute faith in the one transcendent and all-pervasive unity which he affectionately called "My Father." The biography is an inspiring mix of storytelling, interviews and fact-finding.

Hohm Press, Hardback, 30+ photos, 832 pages, $39.95, ISBN: 978-1-890772-35-2

# After Surgery, Illness, or Trauma
*10 Practical Steps to Renewed Energy and Health*
By Regina Sara Ryan,
Foreword by John W. Travis, M.D.

This book fills the important need of helping us survive and even thrive through our necessary "down-time" in recuperating from surgery, trauma, or illness. Whether you are recovering at home or in the hospital for a few days, weeks, or even months, this book will be your guide to a more balanced and even productive recovery. It follows a wellness-approach that addresses: managing and reducing pain; coping with fear, anger, frustration and other unexpected emotions; inspiration for renewed life, becoming an active participant in your own healing; dealing with well-meaning visitors and caregivers ... and more.

Kalindi Press, Paper, 285 pages, $14.95, ISBN: 978- 0-934252-95-9

# OTHER TITLES FROM HOHM PRESS

## As It Is
*A Year on the Road with a Tantric Teacher*
by M. Young

A first-hand account of a one-year journey around the world in the company of *tantric* teacher Lee Lozowick. This book catalogues the trials and wonders of day-to-day interactions between a teacher and his students, and presents a broad range of his teachings given in seminars from San Francisco, California to Rishikesh, India. *As It Is* considers the core principles of *tantra*, including non-duality, compassion (the Bodhisattva ideal), service to others, and transformation within daily life. Written as a narrative, this captivating book will appeal to practitioners of *any* spiritual path. Readers interested in a life of clarity, genuine creativity, wisdom and harmony will find this an invaluable resource.

Paper, 848 pages, 24 b&w photos, $29.95, ISBN: 978-0-934252-99-7

## Feast or Famine
*Teachings on Mind and Emotions*
by Lee Lozowick

This book focuses on core issues related to human suffering: the mind that doesn't "Know Thyself," and the emotions that create terrifying imbalance and unhappiness. The author, a spiritual teacher for over 35 years, details the working of mind and emotions, offering practical interventions for when they are raging out of control. A practical handbook for meditators and anyone dedicated to "work on self." Lee Lozowick has written over twenty books, including: *Conscious Parenting; The Alchemy of Transformation;* and *The Alchemy of Love and Sex;* and has been translated and published in French, German, Spanish, Portuguese and other languages.

Paper, 256 pages, $19.95, ISBN: 978-1-890772-79-6

## Self Observation ~ The Awakening Of Conscience
*An Owner's Manual*
by Red Hawk

This book is an in-depth examination of the much needed process of "self" study known as self observation. It offers the most direct, non-pharmaceutical means of healing the attention dysfunction which plagues contemporary culture. Self observation, the author asserts, is the most ancient, scientific, and proven means to develop conscience, this crucial inner guide to awakening and a moral life.

This book is for the lay-reader, both the beginner and the advanced student of self observation. No other book on the market examines this practice in such detail. There are hundreds of books on self-help and meditation, but almost none on self-study via self observation, and none with the depth of analysis, wealth of explication, and richness of experience that this book offers.

Paper, 160 pages, $14.95, ISBN: 978-1-890772-92-5

## Yearning For The Father
*The Lord's Prayer and the Mystic Journey*
by John Sack

John Sack takes the Lord's Prayer to a whole new level, offering it as a matrix for the contemplative and mystical life. He draws upon history, literature, poetry and his first-hand appreciation of other religious traditions in presenting an extended guidebook to meditation upon these universal and much loved words of Jesus. *Yearning for the Father* illumines the spiritual road map laid out in the prayer: through a series of reflections it explores each phrase of the prayer, aiming always at deeper levels of appreciation. It also considers the place of this proto-typal verbal prayer alongside mental and contemplative prayer.

Paper, 240 pages, $17.95, ISBN: 978-1-890772-55-0

# Grace and Mercy in Her Wild Hair
*Selected Poems to the Mother Goddess*
by Ramprasad Sen
Translated by Leonard Nathan and Clinton Seely

Ramprasad Sen, a great devotee of the Mother Goddess, composed these passionate poems in 18th-century Bengal, India. His lyrics are songs of praise or sorrowful laments addressed to the great goddesses Kali and Tara, guardians of the cycles of birth and death.

Paper, 120 pages, $12, ISBN: 978- 0-934252-94-2

# Marrow Of Flame
*Poems of the Spiritual Journey*
by Dorothy Walters
Foreword by Andrew Harvey

This compilation of 105 new poems documents and celebrates the au-thor's interior journey of *kundalini* awakening. Her poems cut through the boundaries of religious provincialism to the essence of longing, love and union that supports every authentic spiritual tradition, as she writes of the Mother Goddess, as well as of Krishna, Rumi, Bodhidharma, Hildegard of Bingen, and many others. Best-selling spiritual author and poet Andrew Harvey has written the book's Introduction. His commentary illuminates aspects of Dorothy's spiritual life and high-lights the "unfailing craft" of her poems.

"Dorothy Walters writes poetry that speaks to us from the heart to the heart, gently touching our deepest spiritual stirrings."—Riane Eisler, author, *The Chalice and the Blade.*

Paper, 156 pages, $12.00, ISBN: 978-0-934252-96-6

# The Perfection of Nothing
*Reflections on Spiritual Practice*
by Rick Lewis

With remarkable clarity, reminiscent of the early writing of J. Krishnamurti or Alan Watts, Rick Lewis weaves practical considerations about spiritual life with profound mystical understanding. Whether describing the "illusion of unworthiness" that most of us suffer, the challenges of spiritual practice, or his own awe in discovering the majesty of the present moment, this book is full of laser-sharp analogies that make complex philosophical/religious ideas attractive and easy to understand. His nonsectarian approach will be appreciated by seekers and practitioners of any religious tradition¾whether they are actively engaged in spiritual work, or approaching it for the first time. His words provide guidance and inspiration for revealing the spiritual in everyday life.

Paper; 180 pages, $14.95, ISBN: 978-1-890772-02-4

# About the Author

**Regina Sara Ryan** has studied contemplation and mysticism for over forty years. Leaving a Catholic convent where she lived and worked as a nun during the 1960s, she began to explore many religious traditions, particularly inspired by the lives of the great women of Hinduism, Christianity, Buddhism and Sufism. Since meeting her own spiritual mentor, the Western Baul master Lee Lozowick in 1984, Regina has continued to follow what she calls a path of "unashamed devotion" in which she works to bring her life of contemplation into action. She has written in the field of spiritual life, including *The Woman Awake* and *Igniting the Inner Life*, as well as in holistic health and wellness, *The Wellness Workbook* (coauthored with John W. Travis, M.D.). Regina conducts seminars and retreats in the U.S. and Europe. She lives with her husband in Paulden, Arizona.

**Contact:** c/o Hohm Press, PO Box 31, Prescott, Arizona, USA; 928-778-9189; hppublisher@cableone.net

# About Hohm Press

**Hohm Press** is committed to publishing books that provide readers with alternatives to the materialistic values of the current culture, and promote self-awareness, the recognition of interdependence, and compassion. Our subject areas include parenting, religious studies, women's studies, the arts and poetry.

**Contact:** Hohm Press, PO Box 31, Prescott, Arizona, USA; 928-778-9189; hppublisher@cableone.net
**Visit Hohm Press online at www.hohmpress.com**